D1097445

ADVENTURES IN MOCHI-MOCHI LAND

· TALL TALES FROM A TINY KNITTED WORLD ·

ANNA HRACHOVEC

Photographs by Brandi Simons

POTTER
CRAFT

new york

HILLSBORO PUBLIC LIBRARIES
WITHDRAWN
Hillsboro, OR
Member of Washington County
COOPERATIVE LIBRARY SERVICES

Copyright © 2015 by Anna Hrachovec
Photographs on pages 2–95 copyright © 2015 by Brandi Simons
All other photographs copyright © 2015 by Anna Hrachovec

All rights reserved.

Published in the United States by Potter Craft,
an imprint of the Crown Publishing Group,
a division of Random House LLC, a Penguin
Random House Company, New York.
www.pottercraft.com
www.crownpublishing.com

POTTER CRAFT and colophon is a registered
trademark of Random House LLC.

Library of Congress Cataloging-in-Publication Data
is available upon request.

ISBN 978-0-385-34459-3
eBook ISBN 978-0-385-34460-9

Printed in China

5653 9918 07/15 For John

The author and publisher would like to thank the Craft
Yarn Council of America for providing the yarn weight
icons used in this book. For more information,
please visit www.YarnStandards.com.

Text and cover design by Ashley Tucker
Cover photographs by Brandi Simons
and Anna Hrachovec

10 9 8 7 6 5 4 3 2 1
First Edition

Hellooo, and welcome to Mochimochi Land!

A magical place where everything, from the trees to the microwaves, is alive and squishy.

Odd things happen every day in Mochimochi Land, but as a brave adventurer, I've explored its very strangest corners to bring you the very silliest stories. Stick around, and I'll even show you how to knit these cute characters yourself!

Let's begin with a treat of a tale, in which I witnessed the most extraordinary of culinary skills . . .

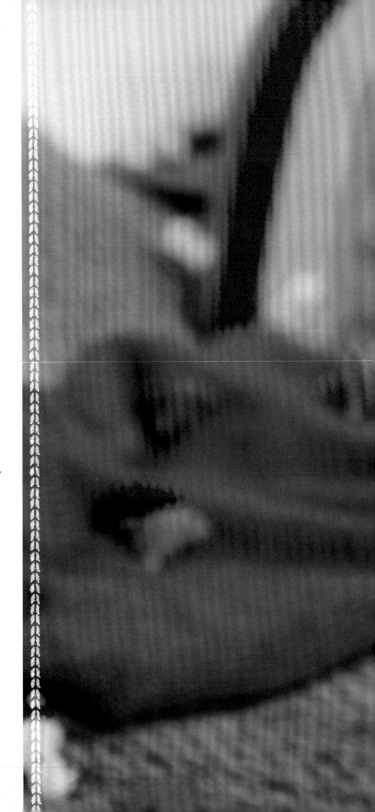

THE hungry
DONUT

It all started in Ovenston, a suburb of Sweet City, the edible capital of Mochimochi Land.

Ovenston is historically a pastry town—half the townspeople are bakers by trade, and the other half are oven repair technicians. Together, they supply all of Mochimochi Land with fresh baked goods.

Biscuit the baker, who specializes in donut holes, wanted to stand out among the Ovenstonians by baking something truly unique.

BISCUIT'S BAKERY
fresh donut holes all day

fresh ingredients

microwaved to perfection

One day it hit her: she would invent the ultimate donut!

When the donut holes in her shop weren't looking, Biscuit snuck out to a cave hidden deep in the Muffin Mountains.

$\int$he plucked a hair
from a sleeping gum-
gum bear, the district's
fiercest delicacy.

Back in her bakery . . .

Biscuit spliced the bear's hair with a sprinkle from one of the donut holes . . .

She put the concoction in the microwave . . .

And before she could brew a pot of coffee, the microwave exploded!

Leaving behind a very large, very bouncy donut.

Success! Only, as Biscuit leaned in to take a bite of her epic experiment, it bounced onto the bakery counter and gobbled up all the other pastries!

Then it rolled right out the door.

Her first mistake was not having a door that locked from the inside. Baked goods are always trying to escape in Mochimochi Land.

The donut wheeled down the block and ate a mallow bunny that was frolicking in the gooey bun bushes.

Then it polished off the gooey bun bushes.

It stopped by Milky Marsh for a drink and
gulped down half of its contents.

Then it careened downtown,

devouring a pie manhole cover . . .

. . . and then a whole lollipop lamppost!

The local bakers looked on in terror as the donut grew to humongous proportions and threatened to consume all of Sweet City.

Even though Biscuit was secretly happy that her bakery would now be famous, she also saw that her hometown was in danger. Something had to be done.

Biscuit gathered the other bakers in town
to formulate a different kind of recipe.

An hour later, they were headed
to Milky Marsh with a truckload
of aromatic coffee beans.

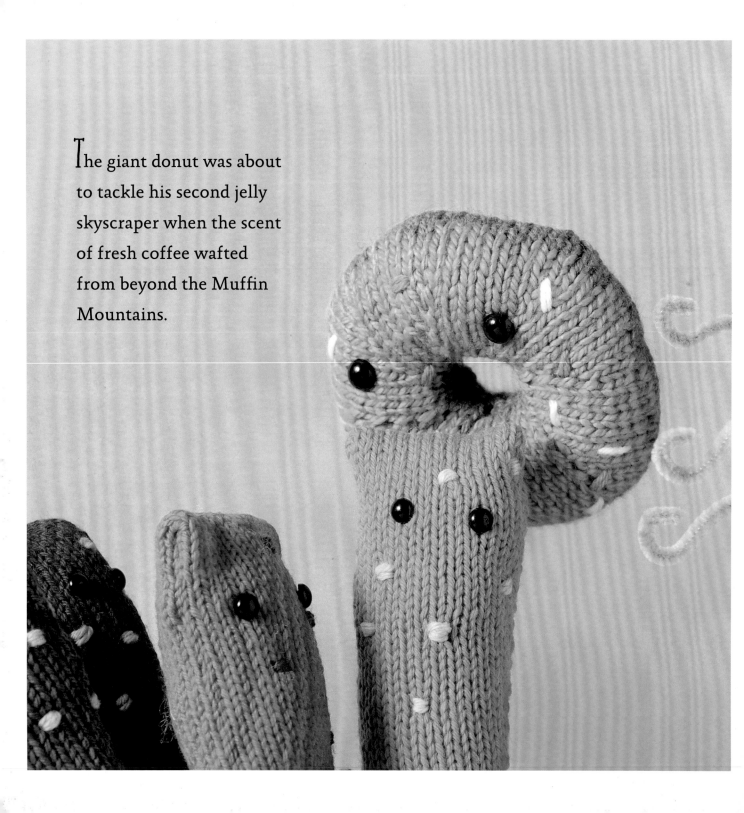

The giant donut was about
to tackle his second jelly
skyscraper when the scent
of fresh coffee wafted
from beyond the Muffin
Mountains.

Instinct took over, and the donut rolled away
from the city center and toward Milky Marsh.

The bakers poured the last
of the coffee beans into the
marsh, which had taken on
a creamy latte-brown color.
They all recognized the
rumble of colossal pastry
on the move . . .

A short while later, the donut
appeared and jumped into
the coffee-filled marsh with
an epic splash!

The bakers rejoiced as the donut began to sink and quickly dissolved into pieces.

But then another thundering sound grew louder—the fragrant coffee and the smell of giant donut had woken up the hibernating gum-gum bears!

The panicked bakers took off running just as the hungry bears reached the marsh.

And thus Mochimochi Land was saved from destruction by gluten, Latte Lake was formed, and the Bakers Dozen Half Marathon was born.

If that story whetted your appetite for Mochimochi wackiness, just wait until you hear about the time the sea creatures held their first election. Who knew that fish could engage in political discourse?

THE underwater ELECTION

Deep in the Soggy Sea, crabs,
dolphins, and other oddly shaped
creatures live peacefully side by side,
and the only complaint anyone
ever has is about the humidity.
At least that's how
things normally are.

The dolphins and the crabs were playing their weekly game of Kick the Puffer. (That might sound cruel, but the puffer also gets to be the referee!)

The crabs were up by six hundred points. The dolphins
had control of the puffer and were about to score . . .

But the octopus
goalie head-butted
the puffer . . .

throwing it off course,
deep into a kelp forest.

When the players found their deflated puffer, she was lying against something big and shiny.

A treasure chest bursting with glittery gold and jewels!

Before anyone could get their fins on it, a dolphin named Bubbles swam front and center. She declared that the dolphins would be in charge because they were the smartest creatures in the sea. "First of all," she said, "we will have a treasure tax, which—ouch!"

Gary, the crabbiest crab in the community, interrupted her. "Oh, no, you don't," he said. "I've had enough of you elitist mammals and your slippery ideas. Anyone who tries to steal this treasure is getting a pinch from me."

A fight was about to break out when the puffer wheezed, "Let's have a vote!"

Gary kicked off his campaign by judging a
beauty contest, with prizes provided by
the treasure.

Bubbles cut the ribbon on a new sandcastle development.
It was two months ahead of schedule, thanks to the treasure's
financial backing.

Gary (and the treasure)
sponsored a litter scavenge
in the shallows.

Soggy Sea Pride

Bubbles threw a huge parade, with the help of you-know-what.

The next day, Bubbles and Gary went head to head in a live debate. The whole sea was in attendance.

The evening started out civilly,
with vague campaign promises.

"If I'm treasurer, everyone will get to swim in the treasure for fifteen minutes each week," Bubbles declared.

"If I'm treasurer," said Gary, "I pledge to build a big net to keep the freshwater from contaminating our salt water. We all know that freshwater fish are the treasure-stealing kind."

But soon things took a negative turn.

"Bubbles, here, is an air breather," Gary said. "All that excess oxygen has made her full of hot air."

"My opponent says he will protect the treasure, but can you really trust someone with eight legs?" asked Bubbles. "He could be crossing four of them behind his back and we'd never know!"

Before long, the debate had devolved into a
mudslinging extravaganza.

No one came out looking clean.

Finally, it was election day. One by one, the Soggy Sea citizens cast their ballots.

The octopi counted the votes
eight times each.

A winner had been chosen! But it was
neither Bubbles nor Gary.

It was the treasure chest! The sea had decided that the chest was already doing a great job of keeping the treasure safe—at least what was left of it.

The candidates' hopes were dashed. But the
puffer knew how to raise their spirits.

And so the richest Kick the Puffer league was established, complete with new uniforms and a cheer squad. Clearly, fiscal responsibility hadn't reached the sea floor. But they were already so far underwater, it hardly made a difference.

THE lighthearted LOVERS

Beyond the Soggy Sea, past the Woolly Woods, Carnivalville operates 24/7. It's known as the most fun and the least safe birthday party destination in Mochimochi Land.

One sunny day, the balloon-selling elephant was waiting for customers and thinking about how he would like to buy a boat someday. Unbeknownst to him, the balloons he was holding were also thinking about getting away.

They'd had enough carnival fun and were ready for an adventure that didn't involve being tied to a sticky kid's wrist.

As luck would have it, the balloon vendor
sneezed out a big "ACHOOF!" and the balloons
saw their chance. They sailed into the sky
before their boss could catch them.

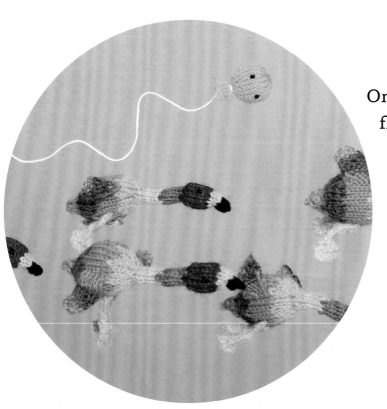

One balloon joined a
flock of rainbowbirds
flying south.

Another balloon
flew too close
to the sun.

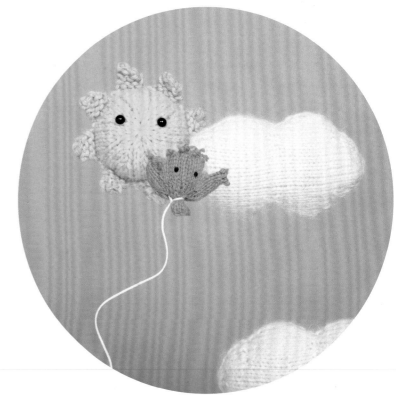

Two balloons
raced a kite . . .
and tied for first!

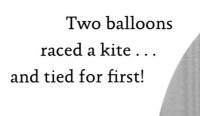

One balloon gave
an earthworm the
ride of his life.

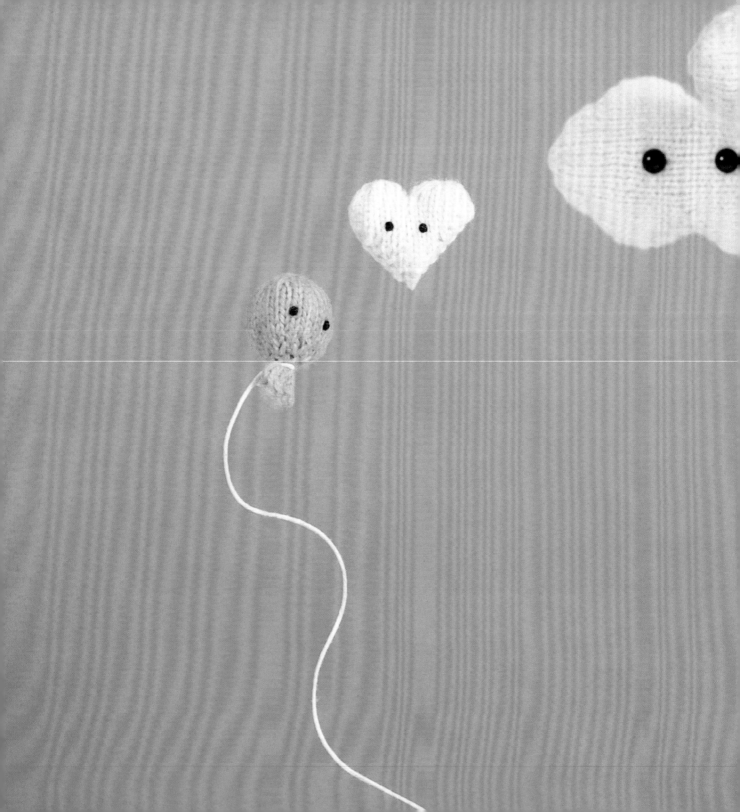

And the last balloon, named Hugo,
fell in love with a blimp.

Her name was A-1. Or at least that's
what was printed on her side.

At first A-1 didn't notice Hugo,
but he drifted up close to her
ear to compliment her on her
buoyancy and speed . . .

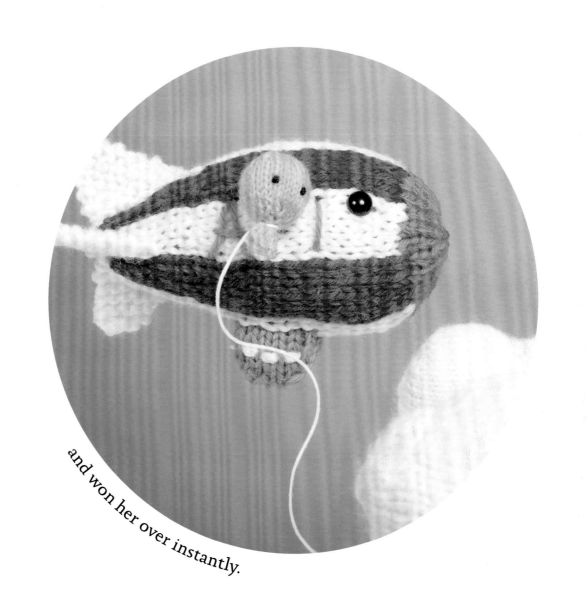

and won her over instantly.

Together Hugo and A-1 drifted all over
Mochimochi Land.

They spotted Gary
riding Bubbles through
the waves below . . .

. . . the bakers racing up
the Muffin Mountains . . .

. . . and the gum-gum bears taking a post-donut nap in the sun.

"C'mon, let's wake them up!" A-1 said, and swooped down quickly.

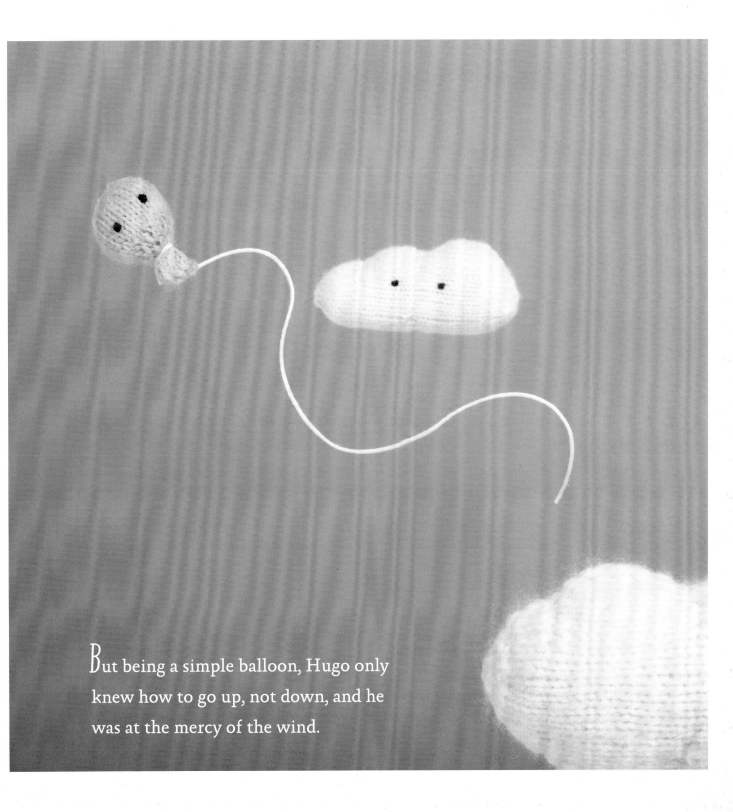

But being a simple balloon, Hugo only knew how to go up, not down, and he was at the mercy of the wind.

A-1 suddenly found herself all alone.

And the sky seemed so empty.

A-1 looked for her love as long as she could,
but the sun hadn't seen him.

Neither had the clouds.

Running low on helium, A-1 was about
give up, when she spotted something
colorful in the distance.

"Head south!" the rainbowbird cried
as he zoomed past.

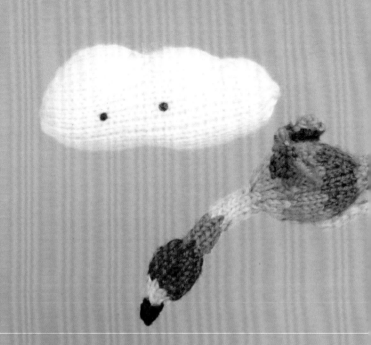

With her last remaining helium supply, A-1 turned and drifted south as straight as she could over the open ocean. She heard a joyful racket coming from a tiny island below.

There was Hugo, along with six
of his fellow balloons, a flock of
rainbowbirds, and more coconut
punch drinks than you could count.

It was a spring break party! A rainbowbird had found Hugo drifting and took him to join his friends.

Another rainbowbird returned with a fresh tank of helium, so everyone could stay up—literally—until dawn.

The End

Now that you've heard my incredible stories,

maybe you think I'm the one who's full of gas. Well, if you say I'm lying, then I challenge you to knit the characters yourself and see what strange adventures happen. Just turn the page to get started!

25 Patterns to Knit Your Own Adventures

Ichigo the Adventurer

finished size

• 1¼" (3cm) tall (not including hat)

special techniques

• Picking up stitches
• 3-needle bind-off

yarn

• Fingering-weight yarn in 5 colors, plus small amount of black
• Samples knit with Knit Picks Palette, 100% wool, 1¾ oz (50g), 231 yds (211m) in Suede **(A)**, Cream **(B)**, Blush **(C)**, Bison **(D)**, Rouge **(E)**, and Black

other supplies

• Set of size 1 US (2.25mm) double-pointed needles
• Small amount of stuffing
• Small tapestry needle

NOTE: The finished project is very small and is not suitable for children ages three and under.

legs

With A, cast on 4 stitches onto one DPN.

Knit 3 rows as an I-cord.

Break the yarn and set the stitches aside on the needle.

Make another leg in the same way as the first, without breaking the yarn.

join legs

Hold the legs parallel on the 2 DPNs, with the purl stitches facing each other and the working yarn attached to the rightmost stitch on the back needle.

Hold the I-cord legs parallel to each other on the needles to get ready to join them in a round.

RND 1: Knit the legs together into one round, starting by knitting the stitches on the front needle, then turning the needles around together to knit the stitches on the other needle (8 sts).

RND 2 (ALSO WORKED ON 2 DPNS): [Kfb] 8 times (16 sts).

body

Distribute the 16 stitches onto 3 DPNs to continue working in a round.

RNDS 3 AND 4: Knit.

Switch to B.

RNDS 5–9: Knit (5 rnds).

Switch to C.

RND 10: Knit.

RND 11: [Kfb, k3] 4 times (20 sts).

RNDS 12–17: Knit (6 rnds).

RND 18: [K2tog, k3] 4 times (16 sts).

RND 19: Knit.

Stuff the piece.

RND 20: [K2tog] 8 times (8 sts).

Break the yarn and draw it tightly through the stitches with a tapestry needle.

With black, embroider eyes onto the face, with two small horizontal stitches for each, placing them 4 stitches up from the last color change and spacing them 3 stitches apart.

arms

With B, cast on 2 stitches onto one DPN.

Knit 18 rows as an I-cord, then break the yarn and draw it tightly through the stitches with a tapestry needle.

With the tail still threaded on the tapestry needle, insert the I-cord through the sides of the body, 2 stitches below the last color change and 1½ stitches to the outside of the eyes. Pull the I-cord halfway through, so that an equal length sticks out from each side. *(See I-Cord Arms on page 136.)*

Weave the loose ends back through the I-cord and body.

hat

With A, cast on 32 stitches onto 3 DPNs and join to work in a round.

RND 1: Knit.

RND 2: [K2tog, k2] 8 times (24 sts).

RND 3: Knit.

RND 4: [K2tog, k4] 4 times (20 sts).

RNDS 5–7: Knit (3 rnds).

RND 8: [K2tog, k3] 4 times (16 sts).

RND 9: Knit.

RND 10: [K2tog] 8 times (8 sts).

Break the yarn and draw it tightly through the stitches with a tapestry needle.

bag

With D, cast on 10 stitches onto 3 DPNs and join to work in a round.

Knit 5 rounds.

Divide the stitches onto 2 DPNs and bind off with a 3-needle bind-off.

Next, with D, pick up and knit 2 stitches at one corner of the cast-on edge.

Knit 20 rows as an I-cord.

Break the yarn, leaving a tail for attaching, and draw it tightly through the stitches with a tapestry needle.

With the tail still threaded on the tapestry needle, stitch the end of the I-cord to the opposite corner of the cast-on edge of the bag.

finishing

With E, embroider loops onto the top of the head by making random loose stitches.

Weave in the loose ends.

Biscuit the Baker

finished size

- 1¼" (3cm) tall (not including hat)

yarn

- Fingering-weight yarn in 4 colors, plus small amount of black **1**

- Sample knit with Cascade Heritage, 75% wool, 25% nylon, 3½ oz (100g), 437 yds (399.5m) in 5625 Purple Hyacinth **(A)**, 5618 Snow **(B)**, 5643 Sunflower **(C)**, 5644 Lemon **(D)**, and 5672 Real Black

other supplies

- Set of size 1 US (2.25mm) double-pointed needles

- Small amount of stuffing

- Small tapestry needle

NOTE: The finished project is very small and is not suitable for children ages three and under.

legs

With A, cast on 4 stitches onto one DPN.

Knit 2 rows as an I-cord.

Break the yarn and set the stitches aside on the needle.

Make another leg in the same way as the first, without breaking the yarn.

join legs

Hold the legs parallel on the 2 DPNs, with the purl stitches facing each other and the working yarn attached to the rightmost stitch on the back needle.

Hold the I-cord legs parallel to each other on the needles to get ready to join them in a round.

RND 1: Knit the legs together into one round, starting by knitting the stitches on the front needle, then turning the needles around together to knit the stitches on the other needle.

RND 2 (ALSO WORKED ON 2 DPNS): [Kfb] 8 times (16 sts).

body

Distribute the 16 sts onto 3 DPNs to continue working in a round.

RND 3: [Kfb, k1] 8 times (24 sts).

Switch to B.

RNDS 4–10: Knit (7 rnds).

Switch to C.

RND 11: [K2tog, k1] 8 times (16 sts).

RND 12: [Kfb, k3] 4 times (20 sts).

RNDS 13–16: Knit (4 rnds).

RND 17: [K2tog, k3] 4 times (16 sts).

RND 18: Knit.

Stuff the piece.

RND 19: [K2tog] 8 times (8 sts).

Break the yarn and draw it tightly through the stitches with a tapestry needle.

With black, embroider eyes onto the face, with two small horizontal stitches for each, placing them 4 stitches up from the last color change and spacing them 2½ stitches apart.

arms

With B, cast on 2 stitches onto one DPN. Knit 18 rows as an I-cord, then break the yarn and draw it tightly through the stitches with a tapestry needle.

With the tail still threaded on the tapestry needle, insert the I-cord through the sides of the body, 2 stitches below the last color change and 1½ stitches to the outside of the eyes. Pull the I-cord halfway through, so that an equal length sticks out from each side. *(See I-Cord Arms on page 136.)*

Weave in the loose ends back through the I-cord and body.

hat

With B, cast on 12 stitches onto 3 DPNs, leaving a tail for attaching, and join to work in a round.

RNDS 1–5: Knit.

RND 6: [Kfb] 12 times (24 sts).

RND 7: Knit.

RND 8: [Kfb, k2] 8 times (32 sts).

RNDS 9 AND 10: Knit.

RND 11: [K2tog] 16 times (16 sts).

RND 12: Knit.

Stuff the top of the piece only.

RND 13: [K2tog] 8 times.

Break the yarn and draw it tightly through the stitches with a tapestry needle. Insert the tail end down through the top of the closed-up stitches, and stitch in place to make the top of the hat flat.

finishing

Weave in all loose ends on the body. With A, embroider 6 buttons onto the torso with 2 small horizontal stitches for each, in 2 columns placed just to the outside of each eye.

Cut a long piece of D, and use it to stitch long, loose loops onto the top of the head.

Stitch loose loops at the top of the head before gathering them into a ponytail.

Once you have made 6 loops or so, gather them at the side of the head and tie them with a piece of A for a ponytail. Cut the loops and trim the hair.

Attach the cast-on edge of the hat to the top of the head with a few small stitches.

Gum-Gum Bear

finished size

- 2" (5cm) tall

special technique

- Picking up stitches

yarn

- Fingering-weight yarn in one color, plus small amounts of white and black
- Sample knit with Cascade Heritage, 75% wool, 25% nylon, 3½ oz (100g), 437 yds (399.5m) in 5628 Cotton Candy (main color), 5618 Snow, and 5672 Real Black

other supplies

- Set of size 1 US (2.25mm) double-pointed needles
- Small amount of stuffing
- Small tapestry needle

NOTE: The finished project is very small and is not suitable for children ages three and under.

body (worked bottom to top)

Cast on 6 stitches of the main color onto 2 DPNs and join to work in a round.

RND 1: [Kfb] 6 times (12 sts).

RND 2: [Kfb, k1] 6 times (18 sts).

Distribute the stitches onto 3 DPNs to continue working in a round.

RND 3: Knit.

RND 4: [Kfb] twice, k5, [kfb] 4 times, k5, [kfb] twice (26 sts).

RND 5: Knit.

RND 6: Kfb, k11, [kfb] twice, k11, kfb (30 sts).

RNDS 7–13: Knit (7 rnds).

RND 14: [K2tog] twice, k7, [k2tog] 4 times, k7, [k2tog] twice (22 sts).

RND 15: [Kfb] twice, k7, [kfb] 4 times, k7, [kfb] twice (30 sts).

RNDS 16–22: Knit (7 rnds).

RND 23: K2tog, k11, [k2tog] twice, k11, k2tog (26 sts).

RND 24: [K2tog] twice, k5, [k2tog] 4 times, k5, [k2tog] twice (18 sts).

RND 25: Knit.

Stuff the piece.

RND 26: [K2tog, k1] 6 times (12 sts).

RND 27: [K2tog] 6 times (6 sts).

Break the yarn and draw it tightly through the stitches with a tapestry needle.

features

Note that the body has a slightly flattened shape; the flat sides will become the front and back of the body. With black, embroider the eyes with 2 small horizontal stitches for each, placing them 8 stitches down from the top of the head and spacing them 4 stitches apart.

Also with black, embroider a mouth with 4 horizontal stitches spanning 3 stitches between and 2 stitches below the eyes. With white, embroider two tiny vertical stitches

onto the top of the mouth for teeth.

With the main color, embroider a nose with 3 horizontal stitches, placed between the eyes and the mouth.

Embroider the ears with 4–6 vertical stitches, placed on either side of the closed-up stitches at the top of the body.

To make the nose and ears, embroider over the same stitches multiple times with the main color to form a 3-dimensional bump.

arms (make 2)

Turn the body upside down, and pick up and knit 4 horizontal stitches at the side of the body, placed on the decrease round at the middle of the body.

ROW 1: Knit one row as an I-cord.

ROW 2 (WORK AS AN I-CORD): [Kfb] 4 times (8 sts).

Divide the stitches onto 2 DPNs to continue working in a round.

RNDS 3–5: Knit (3 rnds).

Insert a pinch of stuffing into the piece.

Break the yarn and draw it tightly through the stitches with a tapestry needle.

Turn the body upside down to pick up the stitches for the arms and legs; make your stitches as close together as possible.

legs (make 2)

With the body still turned upside down, pick up and knit 4 sts to one side of the cast-on stitches.

ROW 1: Knit one row as an I-cord.

ROW 2 (WORK AS AN I-CORD): [Kfb] 4 times (8 sts).

Divide the stitches onto 2 DPNs to continue working in a round.

RNDS 3–6: Knit (4 rnds).

Insert a pinch of stuffing into the piece.

Break the yarn and draw it tightly through the stitches with a tapestry needle.

finishing

Embroider a tail with 4–6 horizontal stitches centered at the bottom back of the body.

Weave in all loose ends.

Growing Donut

finished sizes

• Big donut is 1¾" (4.5cm) in diameter; bigger donut is 3½" (9cm) in diameter; biggest donut is 4¾" (12cm) in diameter

special techniques

• Mattress stitch
• Stranded color knitting

yarn

• **Big donut:** Fingering-weight yarn in 4 colors, plus small amount of black (1)

• Sample knit with Cascade Heritage, 75% wool, 25% nylon, 3½ oz (100g), 437 yds (399.5m) in 5643 Sunflower **(A)**, 5628 Cotton Candy **(B)**, 5626 Turquoise, 5618 Snow, and 5672 Real Black

• **Bigger donut:** Worsted-weight yarn in 4 colors (4)

• Sample knit with Cascade 220, 100% wool, 3½ oz (100g), 220 yds (201m) in 2415 Sunflower **(A)**, 9478 Cotton Candy **(B)**, 9421 Blue Hawaii, and 8505 White

• **Biggest donut:** Chunky yarn in 4 colors (5)

• Sample knit with Cascade 128 Superwash, 100% wool, 3½ oz (100g), 128 yds (117m) in 1982 Harvest Orange **(A)**, 901 Cotton Candy **(B)**, 812 Turquoise, and 871 White

other supplies

• Set of size 1 US (2.25mm) double-pointed needles (for big donut)

• Set of 7" (18cm) size 5 US (3.75mm) double-pointed needles (for bigger donut)

• Set of size 8 US (5mm) double-pointed needles (for biggest donut)

• Stuffing

• Small tapestry needle

• Pair of size 9mm (12mm) safety eyes (for bigger [biggest] donut)

gauge

• **Big donut:** 2" (5cm) = 18 stitches and 25 rows in St st

• **Bigger donut:** 2" (5cm) = 11 stitches and 15½ rows in St st

• **Biggest donut:** 2" (5cm) = 8 stitches and 12 rows in St st

NOTES: The pattern for the three sizes of donut is the same; the different sizes are achieved by changing yarn and needle size.
• If you're knitting for a child aged three or under, replace the safety eyes with embroidered eyes on all three sizes.

Big   Bigger   Biggest

donut

With A, cast on 18 stitches onto 3 DPNs and join to work in a round.

RND 1: Knit.

RND 2: [K2B, k1A] to end.

Switch to B only.

RND 3: [Kfb, k2] 6 times (24 sts).

RND 4: Knit.

RND 5: [M1, k3] 8 times (32 sts).

RND 6: Knit.

RND 7: [M1, k4] 8 times (40 sts).

RND 8: Knit.

RND 9: [M1, k5] 8 times (48 sts).

RND 10: Knit.

RND 11: [M1, k6] 8 times (56 sts).

RND 12: Knit.

RND 13: [M1, k14] 4 times (60 sts).

RND 14: Knit.

RND 15: [K2A, k3B] to end.

Switch to A only.

RNDS 16–18: Knit (3 rnds).

RND 19: [K2tog, k13] 4 times (56 sts).

RND 20: Knit.

RND 21: [K2tog, k5] 8 times (48 sts).

RND 22: Knit.

RND 23: [K2tog, k4] 8 times (40 sts).

RND 24: Knit.

RND 25: [K2tog, k3] 8 times (32 sts).

RND 26: Knit.

RND 27: [K2tog, k2] 8 times (24 sts).

RND 28: Knit.

RND 29: [K2tog, k2] 6 times (18 sts).

RNDS 30 AND 31: Knit.

Bind off all stitches, leaving a tail for seaming.

finishing

Stuff the piece about halfway full, pushing the stuffing into the sides of the piece so that the center holes are clear. Align the cast-on and bound-off stitches, and begin seaming them together using mattress stitch.

When you have a few stitches left to seam together, finish stuffing the piece before completing the seam. For the bigger and biggest donuts, you should also attach the eyes before completing the seam.

For the big donut, embroider the eyes with black using 3 horizontal stitches for each, spacing them 10 stitches apart.

Cut a few inches (centimeters) of the two other colors and embroider sprinkles with a single long stitch for each.

Weave in the loose ends.

To seam the donut's hole, slip the tapestry needle under one cast-on stitch, insert the needle through the donut's hole (turning the piece around and upside down as you do so), then slip the needle under one bound-off stitch. Insert the needle back through the donut's hole, and repeat all the way around the seam.

Mini Microwave

finished size

• 1" (2.5cm) tall

special techniques

• Intarsia
• Mattress stitch
• Picking up stitches
• Wrap + turn

yarn

• Fingering-weight yarn in 2 colors, plus small amounts of 2 contrasting colors and black **1**

• Samples knit with Knit Picks Palette, 100% wool, 1¾ oz (50g), 231 yds (211m) in Pistachio **(A)**, Silver **(B)**, Cream, Orange, and Black

other supplies

• Set of 5 size 1 US (2.25mm) double-pointed needles

• Small tapestry needle

• Small amount of stuffing

NOTE: The finished project is very small and is not suitable for children ages three and under.

top

With A, cast on 8 stitches onto one DPN to work flat.

Beginning with a purl row, work 16 rows of St st.

Instead of turning for the next row, rotate the piece 90 degrees clockwise, and with a second DPN, pick up and knit 11 stitches on the adjacent side. Rotate the piece again and use a third DPN to pick up and knit 8 stitches on the cast-on edge. Finally, use a fourth DPN to pick up and knit 11 more stitches on the remaining side. *(See Picking Up Stitches around the Perimeter of a Piece, page 137.)*

sides

You will proceed by working the 38 stitches in a round using a fifth DPN.

RND 1: Knit.

If it's more comfortable, redistribute the stitches onto 3 DPNs and set the fifth DPN aside.

Beginning with the next round, you will work the piece flat (while keeping the stitches on the DPNs) to incorporate B. Using the wrap + turn technique at the ends of the rows will join the piece together in a round, and you won't have to stitch up a seam later.

ROW 2: K8A, k9B (wrapping A around B once midway through), k21A, then w+t using the first stitch of the round.

ROW 3: P21A, p9B (wrapping A around B once midway through), p8A, then w+t using the last stitch of the round.

ROWS 4–10: Work the previous 2 rows 3 more times, then work Row 2 once more, for 9 total rows of intarsia.

Instead of turning for a purl row after Row 10, continue on to the next stitch to work the piece in the round.

Break B and continue working with A only.

RNDS 11 AND 12: Knit.

bottom

RND 13: K8, BO to end (begin binding off by slipping the 9th stitch over the 10th), and BO the last stitch with the first stitch in the round.

Now you should have 7 stitches on the DPN in your left hand and 1 stitch on the DPN in your right. You will continue by working the piece flat on 2 DPNs.

ROW 14: Knit to the end of the row (8 sts).

ROWS 15–28: Beginning with a purl row, work 14 rows of St st.

Bind off all stitches.

finishing

Fold the bottom flap so that its 3 edges align with the bound-off edge you created in Round 13. Begin seaming the flap to the bound-off edge with mattress stitch. Before finishing the seam, stuff the piece, making sure that the corners are filled out.

With black, embroider the eyes with 2 small horizontal stitches for each, placed midway up the B/window section and spaced 3 stitches apart. Also with black, embroider a handle onto the right side of the window with one long vertical stitch.

With B, embroider a small screen just to the top right of the window with 2 horizontal stitches spanning the width of 2 knit stitches.

With contrasting-color yarn, embroider 2 columns of buttons below the small screen with 2 small horizontal stitches for each.

Weave in the loose ends.

Mallow Bunnies

finished size
- 1¼" (3cm) tall

yarn
- Fingering-weight yarn in one color for each bunny, plus small amount of black
- Samples knit with Knit Picks Palette, 100% wool, 1¾ oz (50g), 231 yds (211m) in Hyacinth, Pistachio, Custard, and Black

other supplies
- Set of size 1 US (2.25mm) double-pointed needles
- Small amount of stuffing
- Small tapestry needle

NOTES: The finished project is very small and is not suitable for children ages three and under. • This project is written to be knit in the round on 2 DPNs. If you get a ladder effect because of this, you can work it on 3 DPNs instead.

body

Cast on 6 stitches onto 2 DPNs and join to work in a round.

RND 1: [Kfb] 6 times (12 sts).

RNDS 2–5: Knit (4 rnds).

RND 6: K1, [k2tog] twice, k2, [k2tog] twice, k1 (8 sts).

Insert a tiny amount of stuffing into the piece.

RND 7: K1, [kfb] twice, k2, [kfb] twice, k1 (12 sts).

RNDS 8–10: Knit (3 rnds).

RND 11: K1, [k2tog] twice, k2, [k2tog] twice, k1 (8 sts).

Insert a tiny amount of stuffing into the top of the piece.

ears

Working with only the 4 stitches on the needle with the working yarn attached, knit 3 rows as an I-cord.

Break the yarn, leaving a tail of 12" (30.5cm).

Thread the tail onto a tapestry needle, and draw the yarn tightly through the stitches of the I-cord you just worked. Next, insert the needle back through the I-cord and reattach the yarn to the leftmost stitch on the remaining DPN. Knit 3 rows as an I-cord, then draw the tail tightly through the stitches. *(See Dividing a Piece into I-Cords, page 136.)*

finishing

With black, embroider eyes with one small horizontal stitch for each, placed 2 stitches below the ears and spaced 2 stitches apart.

Weave in the loose ends.

Gooey Bun

finished size
- ¾" (2cm) tall

special techniques
- Stranded color knitting
- Mattress stitch

yarn
- Fingering-weight yarn in 2 colors, plus small amount of black
- Sample knit with Cascade Heritage, 75% wool, 25% nylon, 3½ oz (100g), 437 yds (399.5m) in 5610 Camel **(A)**, 5618 Snow **(B)**, and 5672 Real Black

other supplies
- Pair of size 1 US (2.25mm) straight or double-pointed needles
- Small tapestry needle
- Small amount of stuffing

NOTE: The finished project is very small and is not suitable for children ages three and under.

gooey bun

With A, cast on 33 stitches onto one needle to work flat.

Beginning with a purl row, work 7 rows of St st.

ROW 8: K2A, [k1B, k3A] to last 3 sts, k1B, k2A.

ROW 9: [P1A, p3B] to last st, p1A.

Switch to B only.

ROWS 10–13: Work 4 rows of St st.

ROW 14: [K1A, k3B] to last st, k1A.

ROW 15: P2A, [p1B, p3A] to last 3 sts, p1B, p2A.

Switch to A only.

ROWS 16–22: Work 7 rows of St st.

Bind off all stitches, and leave a 7" (18cm) tail for seaming.

finishing

Fold the piece in half so that the cast-on and bound-off edges touch and the purl sides face each other.

Using the tail you left when binding off, seam together the cast-on and bound-off edges using mattress stitch. Stuff the piece lightly as you go.

Once you have completed the seam, lay the piece flat on a table and wrap it tightly into a spiral shape. Stitch the piece in place by making several loose stitches that go all the way through the piece in different directions, and stitch flat the open side edge in the process. (Try not to pull the stitches tightly, or else the stitches will pucker.)

With black, embroider the eyes with 2 small horizontal stitches for each one, placed midway up one side and spaced 3 stitches apart.

Weave in the loose ends.

Muffin Mountain

finished size

• 7½" (19cm) tall

special technique

• Whipstitch (see photo)

yarn

• Bulky yarn in 2 colors, plus small amount of accent color **5**

• Sample knit with Cascade 128 Superwash, 100% wool, 3½ oz (100g), 128 yds (117m) in 897 Baby Denim **(A)**, 821 Daffodil **(B)**, and 804 Amethyst

other supplies

• Set of size 8 US (5mm) double-pointed needles

• Size 8 US (5mm) circular needle

• Stuffing

• Tapestry needle

• Two size 15mm safety eyes

NOTES: The muffin top is worked as randomized knit and purl stitches to achieve a fluffy, muffinlike texture. There's no trick to it—simply knit or purl the stitches in the round in a random fashion. For example, one round might be: K3, p2, k1, p4, k4, p2, and so on; and the next round may be: K2, p1, k3, p2, k3, p4, k1, etc.
• If you're knitting for a child aged three or under, replace the safety eyes with embroidered eyes.

wrapper

With A, cast on 4 stitches onto one DPN.

RND 1 (WORK AS AN I-CORD): [Kfb] 4 times (8 sts).

Distribute the stitches onto 3 DPNs to continue working in a round.

RND 2: [Kfb] 8 times (16 sts).

RND 3 AND ALL ODD-NUMBERED RNDS THROUGH RND 17: Purl.

RND 4: [Kfb, p1] 8 times (24 sts).

RND 6: [Kfb, p2] 8 times (32 sts).

RND 8: [Kfb, p3] 8 times (40 sts).

RND 10: [Kfb, p4] 8 times (48 sts).

RND 12: [Kfb, p5] 8 times (56 sts).

Switch to the circular needle now or when it's more comfortable.

RND 14: [Kfb, p6] 8 times (64 sts).

RND 16: [Kfb, p7] 8 times (72 sts).

RNDS 18–39: [K1, p1] to end (22 rnds).

muffin top

Before continuing, cut two 24" (61cm) pieces of B and set them aside for later use.

Switch to B.

RND 40: [K2tog, k4] 12 times (60 sts).

RND 41: [Kfb, k4] 12 times (72 sts).

RND 42: Knit.

RND 43: [Kfb, k5] 12 times (84 sts).

RND 44: Knit.

RND 45: [Kfb, k6] 12 times (96 sts).

RND 46: Knit.

RND 47: [Kfb, k7] 12 times (108 sts).

RNDS 48–53: Work random knit and purl stitches (6 rnds; see pattern note).

Reach inside the piece and pinch together the top of the A section and the bottom of the B section. Using the piece of B that you set aside, whipstitch the 2 layers together around the inside of the piece, making your stitches on the fourth row up or down from the color change. (This will make the muffin top overlap the wrapper.) Use the other piece of B to complete the seam when you run out of the first one.

Use whipstitch around the inside of the piece to make the muffin top overlap the wrapper.

RND 54: [K2tog *or* p2tog, work 7 random stitches] 12 times (96 sts).

RNDS 55 AND 56: Work random knit and purl stitches.

RND 57: [K2tog *or* p2tog, work 14 random stitches] 6 times (90 sts).

RND 58 AND ALL EVEN-NUMBERED RNDS THROUGH RND 84: Work random knit and purl stitches.

RND 59: [K2tog *or* p2tog, work 13 random stitches] 6 times (84 sts).

RND 61: [K2tog *or* p2tog, work 12 random stitches] 6 times (78 sts).

RND 63: [K2tog *or* p2tog, work 11 random stitches] 6 times (72 sts).

RND 65: [K2tog *or* p2tog, work 10 random stitches] 6 times (66 sts).

RND 67: [K2tog *or* p2tog, work 9 random stitches] 6 times (60 sts).

RND 69: [K2tog *or* p2tog, work 8 random stitches] 6 times (54 sts).

Switch back to DPNs now or when they're more comfortable.

RND 71: [K2tog *or* p2tog, work 7 random stitches] 6 times (48 sts).

RND 73: [K2tog *or* p2tog, work 6 random stitches] 6 times (42 sts).

RND 75: [K2tog *or* p2tog, work 5 random stitches] 6 times (36 sts).

Stuff the piece and attach the eyes, placed midway down the wrapper and spaced so that there are 2 columns of knit stitches between them.

RND 77: [K2tog *or* p2tog, work 4 random stitches] 6 times (30 sts).

RND 79: [K2tog *or* p2tog, work 3 random stitches] 6 times (24 sts).

RND 81: [K2tog *or* p2tog, work 2 random stitches] 6 times (18 sts).

If necessary, add more stuffing to the top of the piece.

RND 83: [K2tog *or* p2tog, knit *or* purl] 6 times (12 sts).

RND 85: [K2tog *or* p2tog] 6 times (6 sts).

Break the yarn and draw it tightly through the stitches with a tapestry needle.

finishing

With contrasting-color yarn, embroider fruit specks onto the muffin top with 3–5 stitches for each.

Weave in the loose ends.

Tiny Cherry Pie

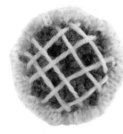

finished size

- 1¼" (3cm) in diameter

special technique

- Back stitch

yarn

- Fingering-weight yarn in 2 colors, plus small amount of black **1**
- Sample knit with Cascade Heritage, 75% wool, 25% nylon, 3½ oz (100g), 437 yds (399.5m) in 5644 Lemon **(A)**, 5647 Flamingo Pink **(B)**, and 5672 Real Black

other supplies

- Set of size 1 US (2.25mm) double-pointed needles
- Small amount of stuffing
- Small tapestry needle

NOTE: The finished project is very small and is not suitable for children ages three and under.

pie (worked bottom to top)

With A, cast on 4 stitches onto one DPN.

RND 1 (WORK AS AN I-CORD): [Kfb] 4 times (8 sts).

Distribute the stitches onto 3 DPNs to continue working in a round.

RND 2: [Kfb] 8 times (16 sts).

RND 3: Knit.

RND 4: [Kfb, k1] 8 times (24 sts).

RND 5: Knit.

RND 6: [Kfb, k2] 8 times (32 sts).

RND 7: Knit.

RND 8: [Kfb, k3] 8 times (40 sts).

RND 9: [Kfb, k9] 4 times (44 sts).

RNDS 10 AND 11: Knit.

RND 12: [K2tog, k9] 4 times (40 sts). Switch to B.

RND 13: [K2tog, k3] 8 times (32 sts).

RND 14: [K1, p1] to end.

RND 15: [K2tog, p1, k1] 8 times (24 sts).

RND 16: P1, [k1, p2] to last 2 sts, k1, p1.

RND 17: [P2tog, k1] 8 times (16 sts).

RND 18: [K1, p1] to end.

Insert a small amount of stuffing into the piece. (Keep in mind that the finished piece should be relatively flat.)

RND 19: [P2tog, k2tog] 4 times (8 sts).

Break the yarn and draw it tightly through the stitches with a tapestry needle. Poke the needle straight down through the bottom of the piece, and make a stitch on the inside bottom of the piece without making a visible stitch on the outside. This will help the piece maintain a flat shape.

finishing

Pinch the piece flat, and use the tails to stitch the shape in place, making sure not to make visible stitches with the opposite side's color.

Use back stitch around the rim of the pie to make a crustlike ridge.

With A, stitch around the rim of the piece using back stitch to form a defined "crust." Make the stitches just to the outside of the color change, and go all the way through the piece with each one.

Also with A, embroider the latticework, weaving the pieces over and under each other as you would a pie crust. Start by making 4 long stitches going in one direction across the piece. Next, make the 4 perpendicular stitches, weaving the tapestry needle alternately over and under the first 4 stitches as you make each stitch.

With black, embroider the eyes in two spaces formed between the latticework, using 2 small horizontal stitches for each.

Weave in the loose ends.

To make the latticework, first make 4 long stitches going in one direction across the top of the piece, then make 4 perpendicular stitches, weaving the tapestry needle alternately over and under the original stitches.

Little Lollipop

finished size
• 4" (10cm) tall

yarn
• Fingering-weight yarn in white and one color, plus small amount of black **1**
• Sample knit with Cascade Heritage, 75% wool, 25% nylon, 3½ oz (100g), 437 yds (399.5m) in 5618 Snow **(A)**, 5647 Flamingo Pink **(B)**, and 5672 Real Black

other supplies
• Set of size 1 US (2.25mm) double-pointed needles
• Small amount of stuffing
• Small tapestry needle
• One white pipe cleaner

NOTE: The finished project is very small and is not suitable for children ages three and under.

stick
With A, cast on 4 stitches onto one DPN.

RND 1 (WORK AS AN I-CORD): [Kfb] 4 times (8 sts).

Divide the stitches onto 2 DPNs to work in a round.

RNDS 2–33: Knit (32 rnds).

Redistribute the stitches onto 3 DPNs.

Carefully insert the pipe

cleaner so that it reaches the bottom of the piece without poking out the bottom. (If the pipe cleaner keeps getting caught in the yarn, try folding the tip back over itself and twisting it gently as you insert it.) Cut the pipe cleaner so that ½" (13mm) sticks out from the top.

Insert a pipe cleaner into the stick section and trim it so that a small bit sticks out from the top.

candy
Switch to B.

RND 34: Knit.

RND 35: [Kfb] 8 times (16 sts).

RND 36: Knit.

RND 37: [Kfb, k1] 8 times (24 sts).

RND 38: Knit.

RND 39: [Kfb, k3] 6 times (30 sts).

RNDS 40–42: Knit (3 rnds).

RNDS 43–45: Purl (3 rnds).

RNDS 46–48: Knit (3 rnds).

RND 49: [K2tog, k3] 6 times (24 sts).

RND 50: Knit.

RND 51: [K2tog, k1] 8 times (16 sts).

RND 52: Knit.

Stuff the candy section of the piece.

RND 53: [K2tog] 8 times (8 sts).

Break the yarn and draw it tightly through the stitches with a tapestry needle.

finishing

With black, embroider the eyes with two small vertical stitches for each one, placed on the purl section and spaced 4 stitches apart.

Weave in the loose ends.

Bubbles the Dolphin

finished size

• 2½" (6.5cm) long

special techniques

• Picking up stitches

• Wrap + turn

yarn

• Fingering-weight yarn in one color, plus small amount of black (1)

• Sample knit with Tosh Merino Light, 100% wool, 4 oz (113g), 420 yds (384m) in Oceana and Black Walnut

other supplies

• Set of 5 size 1 US (2.25mm) double-pointed needles

• Small amount of stuffing

• Small tapestry needle

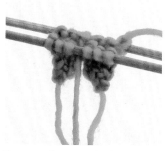

NOTE: The finished project is very small and is not suitable for children ages three and under.

first fin

Cast on 3 stitches onto one DPN.

RND 1 (WORK AS AN I-CORD): [Kfb] 3 times (6 sts).

Divide the stitches onto 2 DPNs to continue working in a round.

RND 2: Knit.

RND 3: K2, [kfb] twice, k2 (8 sts).

RND 4: Knit.

RND 5: K2tog, k4, k2tog (6 sts).

Break the yarn and set the stitches aside on the needles.

second fin

Cast on 3 stitches onto one DPN.

RND 1 (WORK AS AN I-CORD): [Kfb] 3 times (6 sts).

Divide the stitches onto 2 DPNs to continue working in a round.

RND 2: Knit.

RND 3: Kfb, k4, kfb (8 sts).

RND 4: Knit.

RND 5: K2, [k2tog] twice, k2 (6 sts).

join fins

Place the stitches of the first fin that you knit onto the working needles, so that the first 3 stitches of each fin are on the DPN in front and the last 3 stitches of each fin are on the DPN in back, and the working yarn is attached to the rightmost stitch on the back needle.

To get ready to join the fins, place the first 3 stitches of each fin on the front DPN and the last 3 stitches of each fin on the back DPN, with the working yarn attached to the rightmost stitch on the back DPN.

RND 6: Knit one round, joining the fins together as you knit (12 sts).

body

Distribute the stitches onto 3 DPNs to continue working in a round.

RNDS 7 AND 8: Knit.

RND 9: K2, [kfb] twice, k2, kfb, k2, kfb, k2 (16 sts).

RNDS 10 AND 11: Knit.

RND 12: K3, [kfb] twice, k3, kfb, k4, kfb, k2 (20 sts).

RNDS 13 AND 14: Knit.

RND 15: K4, [kfb] twice, k4, kfb, k6, kfb, k2 (24 sts).

RNDS 16 AND 17: Knit.

RND 18: K5, [kfb] twice, k5, kfb, k8, kfb, k2 (28 sts).

RNDS 19–22: Knit (4 rnds).

forehead and snout

RND 23: K1, [k2tog] 3 times, [ssk] 3 times, k15, w+t using the first stitch of the round, p14, w+t, k13, w+t, p12, w+t, k11, w+t, p10, w+t, k12 (22 sts).

RND 24: K8, [k2tog] 3 times, k2, [ssk] 3 times (16 sts).

RND 25: Knit.

Stuff the piece (leaving the fins unstuffed).

RND 26: [K2tog, k2] 4 times (12 sts).

RNDS 27–31: Knit (5 rnds).

Add more stuffing to the end of the piece.

RND 32: [K2tog] 6 times (6 sts).

Break the yarn and draw it tightly through the stitches with a tapestry needle.

With black, embroider the eyes with 2 small horizontal stitches for each,

placed on either side of the head, just behind the w+t round.

Weave in the loose ends.

dorsal fin

Hold the body so that the snout points to the right. Pick up and knit 6 stitches along the middle of the back, placed 4 stitches back from the eyes. You will work these stitches flat.

Pick up the stitches for the dorsal fin in a straight vertical row on the back.

ROW 1: Knit.

ROW 2: Ssk, k4 (5 sts).

ROW 3: Knit.

ROW 4: Ssk, k3 (4 sts).

ROW 5: Knit.

ROW 6: [Ssk] twice, then bind off by slipping the first stitch over the second.

flippers (make 2)

Turn the body upside down, and pick up and knit 3 sts, placed 2 stitches back from and 3 stitches down from one eye. You will work these stitches in the round.

Pick up the 3 stitches for the flippers just below and behind each eye.

RND 1 (WORK AS AN I-CORD): [Kfb] 3 times (6 sts).

Divide the stitches onto 2 DPNs to continue working in a round.

RNDS 2–5: Knit (4 rnds).

Place the stitches together onto one DPN again.

RND 6 (WORK AS AN I-CORD): [K2tog] 3 times (3 sts).

Break the yarn and draw it tightly through the stitches with a tapestry needle (without stuffing the piece).

finishing

Weave in the remaining loose ends.

Gary the Crab

finished size
• 1¼" (3cm) in diameter

special technique
• Picking up stitches

yarn
• Fingering-weight yarn in one color, plus small amount of black
• Sample knit with Tosh Merino Light, 100% wool, 4 oz (113g), 420 yds (384m) in Torchere and Black Walnut

other supplies
• Set of 5 size 1 US (2.25mm) double-pointed needles
• Small amount of stuffing
• Small tapestry needle

NOTE: The finished project is very small and is not suitable for children ages three and under.

body
Cast on 4 stitches onto one DPN.

RND 1 (WORK AS AN I-CORD): [Kfb] 4 times (8 sts).

RND 2: [Kfb] 8 times (16 sts).

Distribute the stitches onto 3 DPNs to continue working in a round.

RND 3: Knit.

RND 4: [Kfb, k1] 8 times (24 sts).

RND 5: Knit.

RND 6: [K2, yo] 3 times, k2, kfb, k6, kfb, k2, [yo, k2] 3 times (32 sts).

RNDS 7 AND 8: Knit.

RND 9: Purl.

RND 10: Knit.

RND 11: [K2tog, k2] 8 times (24 sts).

RND 12: Knit.

RND 13: [K2tog, k1] 8 times (16 sts).

RND 14: Knit.

Insert a pinch of stuffing into the piece. (Stuff lightly enough for the piece to retain a relatively flat shape.)

RND 15: [K2tog] 8 times (8 sts).

Break the yarn and draw it tightly through the stitches with a tapestry needle.

legs
back legs

Cast on 2 stitches onto one DPN.

Knit 14 rows as an I-cord, then break the yarn and draw it tightly through the stitches with a tapestry needle.

With the end still threaded on the tapestry needle, turn the body upside down, and insert the I-cord through the 2 yarn-over holes that are separated by 4 stitches. Pull the I-cord halfway through, so that an equal length sticks out from each side.

Leave the loose ends intact for now. (This will allow the subsequent I-cords to be pulled smoothly through the body.)

middle legs

Work a 2-stitch, 18-row I-cord, and draw it through the next opposing pair of yarn-over holes.

As you make each I-cord pair of legs, insert the I-cord through 2 yarn-over holes on the opposite sides of the body.

front legs

Work a 2-stitch, 20-row I-cord, and draw it through the remaining pair of yarn-over holes.

Weave in all loose ends.

eyes
With black, embroider the eyes with 2 small vertical sts for each one on the purl round, centered between the longest I-cord legs and spaced 4 stitches apart.

claws (make 2)
Turn the body upside down, and pick up and knit 2 stitches, aligned with the legs and just to the outside of one eye.

To get ready to make a claw, turn the body over and pick up and knit 2 stitches to the outside of one eye.

Knit 4 rows as an I-cord.

Turn for the next row.

ROW 5: [Kfb] twice (4 sts).

Turn again, and break the yarn, leaving a tail of a few inches or centimeters.

Thread the tail onto a tapestry needle, and insert the needle through the first 2 stitches from left to right, without slipping the stitches off the DPN. Insert the tapestry needle from left to right through the 2 stitches again, then slip the 2 stitches off the DPN and pull tightly.

Insert the tapestry needle through the tip of the I-cord and reattach the yarn to the next stitch. Repeat what you did with the first 2 stitches, then slip the stitches off the DPN and weave in the loose ends.

Treasure Chest

finished size
- 4" (10cm) wide by 3½" (9cm) tall

special techniques
- Back stitch
- Mattress stitch
- Picking up stitches
- Single crochet stitch (optional, for gold chain) ,
- Stranded color knitting
- 3-needle bind-off

yarn
- Worsted-weight yarn in 2 colors (4) , plus small amounts of sportweight, metallic novelty yarn for treasure (3)
- Sample knit with Berroco Vintage, 52% acrylic, 40% wool, 8% nylon, 3½ oz (100g), 217 yds (198m) in 5167 Dewberry (**A**); Berroco Captiva, 60% cotton, 23% polyester, 17% acrylic, 1¾ oz (50g), 98 yds (90m) in 5556 Vapor (**B**); and Lion Brand Bonbons Metallic, 96% acrylic, 4% metallic polyester, 8 x ⅓ oz (10g), 8 x 38 yds (35m) in various colors

other supplies
- Set of 5 size 5 US (3.75mm) double-pointed needles
- Set of size 2 US (2.75mm) double-pointed needles
- Small tapestry needle
- Small amount of stuffing
- Two size 9mm safety eyes
- Size F-5 (3.75mm) crochet hook (for gold chains) *or* pair of size 5 US (3.75mm) double-pointed needles

NOTES: If you're knitting for a child ages three or under, replace the safety eyes with embroidered eyes. • The bottom half of the chest is worked in the round, but the top half is worked flat, so the color changes in the top piece require you to twist the yarns before working the last stitch in each row. • The smaller size DPNs are only used for the treasure elements and chain. • The pearl from the Joyful Oyster pattern (page 119) may be worked in the sportweight yarn for another treasure element.

base
With A, cast on 11 stitches onto one DPN to work flat.

Beginning with a purl row, work 22 rows of St st.

Instead of turning for the next row, rotate the piece 90 degrees clockwise, and with a second DPN, pick up and knit 16 stitches on the adjacent side. Rotate the piece again and use a third DPN to pick up and knit 11 stitches on the cast-on edge. Finally, use a fourth DPN to pick up and knit 16 more stitches on the remaining side. *(See Picking Up Stitches around the Perimeter of a Piece, page 137.)*

sides
You will proceed by working the 54 stitches in a round using a fifth DPN.

Switch to B (without breaking A).

RNDS 1 AND 2: Knit.

RNDS 3–12: [K1B, k4A] 3 times, k1B, k6A, [k1B, k4A] 4 times, k1B, k6A, k1B, k4A (10 rnds).

Switch to B only (without breaking A).

RNDS 13 AND 14: Knit.

lining

Break B, and continue working with A.

RND 15: Knit.

RND 16: K2tog, k7, [k2tog] twice, k12, [k2tog] twice, k7, [k2tog] twice, k12, k2tog (46 sts).

RNDS 17–28: Knit (12 rnds).

RND 29: [K2tog] twice, k1, [k2tog] 4 times, k6, [k2tog] 4 times, k1, [k2tog] 4 times, k6, [k2tog] twice (30 sts).

RND 30: K1, and move this stitch to the last needle—this will now be the last stitch in the round. Continue knitting to the end of the round.

Stuff the piece about ¼ of the way full, and attach the eyes, placing them 3 stitches down on the vertical stripes of B that are on one of the longer sides.

Divide the stitches onto 2 DPNs and bind off with a 3-needle bind-off, leaving a tail for attaching.

top lining

With A, cast on 20 sts onto one DPN to work flat.

Beginning with a purl row, work 15 rows of St st.

top

Switch to B (without breaking A).

ROW 16: Knit.

ROW 17: Purl.

ROW 18: K2B, k4A, k1B, k6A, k1B, k4A, k2B—twist A once over B before the last stitch.

ROW 19: P2B, p4A, p1B, p6A, p1B, p4A, p2B—twist A once over B before the last stitch.

ROWS 20–35: Repeat the previous 2 rows 8 more times, for 18 total rows of the color pattern.

back flap

Break A, and continue working with B.

ROW 36: Knit.

ROW 37: Purl.

ROW 38: K1, [k2tog] twice, k to last 5 sts, [k2tog] twice, k1 (16 sts).

ROW 39: Purl.

ROW 40: Knit.

ROW 41: Purl.

Bind off the stitches, leaving a tail for seaming.

side panels

With A, pick up and knit 11 stitches along the side edge of the stockinette section of A to work flat.

ROW 1: Purl.

ROW 2: K1, k2tog, k5, k2tog, k1 (9 sts).

ROW 3: Purl.

ROW 4: K1, k2tog, k3, k2tog, k1 (7 sts).

ROW 5: Purl.

ROW 6: K1, k2tog, k1, k2tog, k1 (5 sts).

ROW 7: Purl.

Bind off the stitches.

Rotate the piece around 180 degrees, and pick up and knit 11 stitches along the opposite side from the first 11 that you picked up. Work the same as the other side panel.

top handle

With B, cast on 2 stitches onto one DPN, leaving a tail for attaching, and knit 11 rows as an I-cord.

Break the yarn, leaving a tail for attaching, and draw it tightly through the stitches with a tapestry needle.

side handles (make 2)

With B, cast on 2 stitches onto one DPN, and knit 9 rows as an I-cord.

Break the yarn, leaving a tail for attaching, and draw it tightly through the stitches with a tapestry needle.

finishing

Stuff the lining of the chest bottom inside the rest of the piece, and secure the lining to the bottom of the chest with a few loose stitches.

Fold the chest top over the lining and sides, so that the cast-on edge aligns with the last row of color knitting that you worked. Stitch the cast-on edge to this row using mattress stitch. Next, stitch the side edges of the top around the sides that you picked up using mattress stitch, stuffing the piece before you finish the last seam.

Place the chest top onto the bottom, and attach it to the last row of B on the bottom piece, using mattress stitch.

Attach either end of the top handle to the top of the chest using back stitch, and do the same with the side handles on either side of the chest.

With B, embroider the latch with 3 horizontal stitches and 2 vertical stitches abutting them, between the eyes and on the chest top.

Weave in the loose ends.

gem

With the sportweight yarn, cast on 4 stitches onto one smaller DPN.

RND 1 (WORK AS AN I-CORD): [Kfb] 4 times (8 sts).

Distribute the stitches onto 3 DPNs to continue working in a round.

RNDS 2 AND 3: Knit.

RND 4: Kfb, k2, [kfb] twice, k2, kfb (12 sts).

RND 5: Knit.

RND 6: K2tog, k2, [k2tog] twice, k2, k2tog (8 sts).

RNDS 7 AND 8: Knit.

Insert a pinch of stuffing into the piece.

RND 9: [K2tog] 4 times (4 sts).

Break the yarn and draw it tightly through the stitches with a tapestry needle.

Weave in the loose ends.

chain

With the sportweight yarn, tie a slipknot onto the crochet hook, and work a single chain for as long as you like. *(See Crochet Chain, page 141.)*

Alternatively, cast on one stitch onto a larger DPN, and work a long, loose I-cord for as long as you like.

To finish, break the yarn and draw it through the last loop.

Weave the loose ends through the chain.

Tiny Puffer Fish

finished size
• 1½" (3.8cm) long

special techniques
• Bobble stitch (see box)
• Picking up stitches

yarn
• Fingering-weight yarn in one color, plus small amount of black (1)
• Sample knit with Tosh Merino Light, 100% wool, 4 oz (113g), 420 yds (384m) in Candlewick and Black Walnut

other supplies
• Set of size 1 US (2.25mm) double-pointed needles
• Small amount of stuffing
• Small tapestry needle

NOTE: The finished project is very small and is not suitable for children ages three and under.

> ### special stitch
> **Bobble Stitch:** Knit into the front and back of the stitch twice (making 4 stitches on the right needle), then pass the first 3 increase stitches over the last stitch on the right needle.

body

Cast on 4 stitches onto one DPN.

RND 1 (WORK AS AN I-CORD): [Kfb] 4 times (8 sts).

Distribute the stitches onto 3 DPNs to continue working in a round.

RND 2: [Kfb] 8 times (16 sts).

RND 3: Knit.

RND 4: [M1, k2] 8 times (24 sts).

RNDS 5 AND 6: Knit.

RND 7: [M1, k4] 6 times (30 sts).

RNDS 8–15: Knit (8 rnds).

RND 16: [K2tog, k3] 6 times (24 sts).

RND 17: Knit.

RND 18: K11, bobble1, k5, bobble1, k6.

RND 19: [K2tog, k1] 8 times (16 sts).

Stuff the piece.

RND 20: [K2tog] 8 times (8 sts).

RNDS 21 AND 22: Knit.

Break the yarn and draw it tightly through the stitches with a tapestry needle.

With black, embroider eyes with 2 small horizontal stitches for each, placed just in front of each of the bobbles.

tail fin

Turn the body sideways with the eyes pointed down, and pick up and knit 3 stitches at the cast-on area to work flat.

To begin making the tail fin, turn the body sideways with the eyes pointed down, and pick up and knit 3 stitches at the cast-on area.

Row 1: Knit.

Row 2: K1, kfb, k1 (4 sts).

Row 3: K1, [kfb] twice, k1 (6 sts).

Bind off the stitches.

side fins (make 2)

Turn the body upside down, and pick up and knit 2 sts, placed just below and 4 stitches back from one eye. You will work these stitches flat.

To begin making a side fin, turn the body upside down and pick up and knit 2 stitches, placed 4 stitches back from and just below one eye.

ROW 1: Knit.

ROW 2: [Kfb] twice (4 sts).

Bind off the stitches.

finishing

Weave in the loose ends.

Tiny Octopus

finished size

• 1½" (3.8cm) tall

yarn

• Fingering-weight yarn in one main color, one contrasting color, and a small amount of black (1)

• Sample knit with Tosh Merino Light, 100% wool, 4 oz (113g), 420 yds (384m) in Nassau Blue (main color), Tomato, and Black Walnut

other supplies

• Set of size 1 US (2.25mm) double-pointed needles

• Small tapestry needle

• Small amount of stuffing

• Scrap yarn

NOTE: The finished project is very small and is not suitable for children ages three and under.

legs

With the main color, cast on 3 stitches onto one DPN, leaving a tail of 4" (10cm).

You will work the first 6 rounds as an I-cord.

RND 1: Knit.

RND 2: K1, kfb, k1 (4 sts).

RNDS 3–5: Knit (3 rnds).

RND 6: [Kfb, k1] twice (6 sts).

Divide the stitches onto 2 needles to continue working in a round.

RNDS 7–12: Knit (6 rnds).

Break the yarn, leaving a tail of 5" (12.5cm). Leave the first 3 stitches of the round on the DPN, and slip the last 3 stitches onto an 8" (20cm) strand of scrap yarn.

Make a second leg in the same way as the first one, and place its first 3 stitches onto the same DPN that's holding the stitches from the first leg. Slip the last 3 stitches onto the scrap yarn next to the stitches from the first leg.

Make 5 more legs, and place the first 3 stitches of each onto the DPN, and the last 3 stitches onto the scrap yarn as you make them.

Work the eighth leg the same as the previous 7, without breaking the yarn.

Hold the DPN with the 7 legs facing you, and slip the *last 3 stitches* of the eighth leg onto the left end of the DPN, so that the working yarn is attached to the leftmost stitch of the group.

Slip the *first 3 stitches* of the eighth leg onto the scrap yarn.

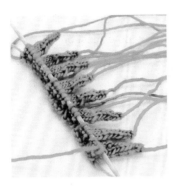

As you finish the first 7 legs, place the first 3 stitches of each one onto a needle and the last 3 stitches of each one onto a piece of scrap yarn alongside the other legs. Leave the working yarn attached to the eighth leg, and place its last 3 stitches onto the left end of the needle and its first 3 stitches onto the scrap yarn.

Tie the 2 ends of the scrap yarn into a circle, and tie all the loose ends together into one large, loose knot. Next, distribute the 24 sts from the DPN onto 3 DPNs to work in a round.

Once all 8 legs are on the needle and scrap yarn, tie the scrap yarn into a circle, tie the loose ends together, and distribute the remaining 24 stitches onto 3 DPNs.

join the legs and work the head

RND 13: Knit, joining the legs together.

RND 14: [K2tog, k2] 6 times (18 sts).

RND 15: [Kfb, k2] 6 times (24 sts).

RNDS 16–23: Knit (8 rnds).

RND 24: [K2tog, k2] 6 times (18 sts).

RNDS 25 AND 26: Knit.

RND 27: [K2tog, k1] 6 times (12 sts).

RND 28: Knit.

RND 29: [K2tog] 6 times (6 sts).

Break the yarn and draw it tightly through the stitches with a tapestry needle.

underside

Turn the piece upside down, and untie the large knot of loose ends. Weave in the 8 loose ends at the cast-on tips of the legs.

Undo or cut the scrap yarn, and transfer the 24 stitches onto 3 DPNs to work in a round, leaving the loose ends on the outside of the piece. Tie the loose ends together into another large, loose knot.

Reattach the yarn to the last stitch on one of the DPNs—this will become the last stitch in the round.

RND 30: Knit.

RND 31: [K2tog, k1] 8 times (16 sts).

RND 32: Knit.

Stuff the head, leaving the legs unstuffed.

RND 33: [K2tog] 8 times (8 sts).

Break the yarn and draw it tightly through the stitches with a tapestry needle.

finishing

Untie the knot of loose ends, and weave all of them in. If you find that there are big gaps between the legs, use these ends to close the gaps with 1–2 stitches for each.

With black, embroider the eyes with 2 small horizontal stitches for each, placed midway up the head and spaced 3½ stitches apart.

With the contrasting color, embroider suckers onto the undersides of the legs with 2 small stitches for each, placed in a random fashion.

Weave in the remaining loose ends.

Soggy Sea Sandcastle

finished size
• 3½" (9cm) tall

special technique
• Mattress stitch

yarn
• Worsted-weight yarn in one main color and a small amount of a contrasting color (4)
• Sample knit with Cascade 220, 100% wool, 3½ oz (100g), 220 yds (200m) in 9463B Gold and 7802 Cerise

other supplies
• Set of size 5 US (3.75mm) double-pointed needles
• Small amount of stuffing
• Small tapestry needle
• Two size 6mm safety eyes
• Straight pins

NOTE: If you're knitting for a child ages three or under, replace the safety eyes with embroidered eyes.

main tower
Cast on 4 stitches onto one DPN.

RND 1 (WORK AS AN I-CORD): [Kfb] 4 times (8 sts).

Distribute the stitches onto 3 DPNs to continue working in a round.

RND 2: [Kfb] 8 times (16 sts).

RND 3: Knit.

RND 4: [Kfb, k1] 8 times (24 sts).

RND 5: Knit.

RND 6: [Kfb, k2] 8 times (32 sts).

RNDS 7–18: Knit (12 rnds).

RND 19: Purl.

RND 20: [P2tog, p2] 8 times (24 sts).

RND 21: [P2tog, p4] 4 times (20 sts).

RNDS 22–27: Knit (6 rnds).

RND 28: [K2tog, k3] 4 times (16 sts).

RNDS 29–31: Knit (3 rnds).

Turn the piece inside out—you will continue to work in a round as you have been, but with the piece growing out away from you instead of toward you.

Before continuing, stuff the piece and attach the eyes, placed 5 stitches down from the knit stitches (which you made by purling) and spaced 4 stitches apart.

After Round 31, turn the piece inside out and continue working in a round.

RND 32: [K2tog, k2] 4 times (12 sts).

RNDS 33 AND 34: Knit.

RND 35: [K2tog, k1] 4 times (8 sts).

RND 36: Knit.

Break the yarn and draw it tightly through the stitches with a tapestry needle.

main parapet
Cast on 30 stitches onto 3 DPNs and join to work in a round.

RNDS 1–6: Knit.

RND 7: [Yo, k2tog] to end.

RNDS 8 AND 9: Knit.

RND 10: [M1, k10] 3 times (33 sts).

RNDS 11–13: Knit (3 rnds).

Bind off all the stitches.

side towers (make 2)
Cast on 6 stitches onto 3 DPNs and join to work in a round.

RND 1: [Kfb] 6 times (12 sts).

RNDS 2–19: Knit (18 rnds).

Turn the piece inside out and stuff it.

RND 20 (WORKED INSIDE OUT): [k2tog] 6 times (6 sts).

Break the yarn and draw it tightly through the stitches with a tapestry needle.

side parapets (make 2)
Cast on 16 sts onto 3 DPNs and join to work in a round.

RNDS 1–4: Knit.

RND 5: [Yo, k2tog] 8 times.

RNDS 6–9: Knit (4 rnds).

Bind off the stitches.

finishing
Fold the parapets in half, so that their yarn-over holes create a picot edge. Place the main parapet around the knit stitches of the main tower, with the bound-off edge of

Joyful Oyster

finished size

• 2½" (6.5cm) tall when closed

special techniques

• Back stitch
• Mattress stitch

yarn

• Worsted-weight yarn in 3 colors, plus small amount of black for the pearl's eyes
• Sample knit with Cascade 220, 100% wool, 3½ oz (100g), 220 yds (200m) in 7802 Cerise **(A)**, 4192 Soft Pink **(B)**, 8010 Natural **(C)**, and 8555 Black

other supplies

• Set of size 5 US (3.75mm) double-pointed needles
• Small amount of stuffing
• Small tapestry needle
• Two size 6mm safety eyes
• Straight pins

NOTE: If you're knitting for a child ages three or under, replace the safety eyes with embroidered eyes.

the parapet facing out. Attach the parapet with several long, loose stitches that go all the way through the piece. Place the side parapets around the side towers, so that the tops of the towers are even with the tops of the parapets, and stitch in place.

Pin the side towers to either side of the main tower, placed so that the main tower sticks out in front and the side towers support it. Attach the side towers to the main tower using mattress stitch, making your stitches only on the parts of the towers that touch directly, so that they are hidden.

Weave in the loose ends.

With the contrasting-color yarn, embroider shells onto the main parapet, with 4 long stitches for each radiating out from a central point.

bottom half

With A (the outer color), cast on 4 stitches onto one DPN.

RND 1 (WORK AS AN I-CORD): [Kfb] 4 times (8 sts).

Distribute the stitches onto 3 DPNs to continue working in a round.

RND 2: [Kfb] 8 times (16 sts).

RND 3: Knit.

RND 4: [M1, k2] 8 times (24 sts).

RND 5: Knit.

RND 6: [M1, k3] 8 times (32 sts).

RNDS 7 AND 8: Knit.

RND 9: [M1, k4] 8 times (40 sts).

RNDS 10 AND 11: Knit.

Switch to B.

RNDS 12 AND 13: Knit.

RND 14: [K2tog, k3] 8 times (32 sts).

RNDS 15 AND 16: Knit.

RND 17: [K2tog, k2] 8 times (24 sts).

RNDS 18 AND 19: Knit.

RND 20: [K2tog, k1] 8 times (16 sts).

RND 21: Knit.

Stuff the piece, making sure that the piece fills out while retaining a relatively flat shape.

RND 22: [K2tog] 8 times (8 sts).

Break the yarn and draw it tightly through the stitches with a tapestry needle.

top half

With A, cast on 4 stitches onto one DPN.

RND 1 (WORK AS AN I-CORD): [Kfb] 4 times (8 sts).

Distribute the stitches onto 3 DPNs to continue working in a round.

RND 2: [Kfb] 8 times (16 sts).

RNDS 3 AND 4: Knit.

RND 5: [M1, k2] 8 times (24 sts).

RNDS 6 AND 7: Knit.

RND 8: [M1, k3] 8 times (32 sts).

RNDS 9 AND 10: Knit.

RND 11: [M1, k4] 8 times (40 sts).

RNDS 12–14: Knit (3 rnds).

Switch to B.

RNDS 15 AND 16: Knit.

RND 17: [K2tog, k3] 8 times (32 sts).

RND 18: Knit.

RND 19: [K2tog, k2] 8 times (24 sts).

RND 20: Knit.

RND 21: [K2tog, k1] 8 times (16 sts).

RND 22: Knit.

Stuff the piece, and attach the eyes, placed 3 stitches above the color change (when you hold the piece upside down with A on top) and spaced 7 stitches apart.

RND 23: [K2tog] 8 times (8 sts).

Break the yarn and draw it tightly through the stitches with a tapestry needle.

flap

Hold the top piece with the A side facing you and the eyes pointing down, and with A, pick up and knit 9 stitches on the top edge to work flat. (Pick up the stitches on the A side of the color change.)

To get ready to make the flap in back, pick up and knit 9 stitches on the edge of the top piece.

ROW 1: K2tog, k5, k2tog (7 sts).

ROWS 2 AND 3: Knit.

ROW 4: Kfb, k5, kfb (9 sts).

Bind off the stitches, leaving a tail for attaching.

shell assembly

Place the top and bottom pieces together with the B sides facing each other. Fold the flap so that it touches the A side of the bottom piece, and attach its bound-off edge to the last row of A stitches on the bottom piece, using mattress stitch.

lips

With A, cast on 2 stitches onto one DPN, leaving a tail of 12" (30cm). Knit an I-cord until it measures 10" (25.5cm). Leave the stitches live on the needle.

Place the cast-on end of the I-cord in one corner of the shell, next to the flap, and pin in place. Pin the rest of the I-cord in a wavy pattern to the shell, with the peaks of the wave touching the third row of stitches on the A side and the valleys touching the first row of stitches on the B side.

Before finishing off the I-cord, pin it to the shell in a wavy pattern while the stitches are still live on the needle.

Adjust the I-cord length by adding or taking out stitches—when you have the correct length, break the yarn and pull it loosely through the stitches with a tapestry needle.

Using the tail that you left when casting on, begin stitching the I-cord to the shell in a wavy pattern using back stitch. Remove the pins as you come to them. When you reach the end of the I-cord, make any final adjustments to its length, then pull the last 2 stitches tightly.

Make another I-cord with A, adjusting the length based on the first one that you knit. Attach it to the other half of the shell in the same way as above.

Weave in the loose ends.

pearl

With C, cast on 6 stitches onto 3 DPNs and join to work in a round.

RND 1: [Kfb] 6 times (12 sts).

RNDS 2–5: Knit (4 rnds).

Insert a pinch of stuffing into the piece.

RND 6: [K2tog] 6 times (6 sts).

Break the yarn and draw it tightly through the stitches with a tapestry needle.

With black, embroider eyes onto the pearl with two small horizontal stitches for each, spaced 1½ stitches apart.

Weave in the loose ends.

Tiny Balloons

finished size

- 1¼" (3cm) tall (not including string)

yarn

- Fingering-weight yarn in 3 colors, plus white and black (1)
- Samples each knit with Knit Picks Palette, 100% wool, 1¾ oz (50g), 231 yds (211m) in Canary, Serrano, or Cyan, plus White and Black

other supplies

- Set of size 1 US (2.25mm) double-pointed needles
- Small amount of stuffing
- Small tapestry needle

Note: The finished project is very small and is not suitable for children ages three and under.

balloon

Cast on 8 stitches onto 2 DPNs. Hold the DPNs parallel, with the working yarn attached to the rightmost stitch on the back DPN, to work in a round.

RNDS 1 AND 2: Knit.

RND 3: [K2tog] 4 times (4 sts).

RND 4: [Kfb] 4 times (8 sts).

RND 5: Knit.

RND 6: [Kfb] 8 times (16 sts).

Distribute the stitches onto 3 DPNs to continue working in a round.

RNDS 7 AND 8: Knit.

RND 9: [M1, k2] 8 times (24 sts).

RNDS 10–15: Knit (6 rnds).

RND 16: [K2tog, k1] 8 times (16 sts).

RND 17: Knit.

Stuff the piece.

RND 18: [K2tog] 8 times (8 sts).

Break the yarn and draw it tightly through the stitches with a tapestry needle.

finishing

With black, embroider eyes with 2 small horizontal stitches for each, placed midway up one side and spaced 3 stitches apart. (If stitching together a group of balloons, do this step after all of the balloons are attached.)

Weave in the loose ends.

Cut a 4" (10cm) long piece of white yarn, and tie one end around the skinny part of the balloon.

To stitch a group of balloons together, begin by attaching 2 balloons together with 2–3 small stitches. As you add more balloons, stitch them together wherever they touch each other.

Carnie Elephant

finished size
• 2" (5cm) tall

special techniques
• Picking up stitches
• Stranded color knitting

yarn
• Fingering-weight yarn in 5 colors, plus small amount of black
• Sample knit with Knit Picks Palette, 100% wool, 1¾ oz (50g), 231 yds (211m) in Silver (A), White (B), Cyan (C), Canary (D), Serrano (E), and Black

other supplies
• Set of 5 size 1 US (2.25mm) double-pointed needles
• Small amount of stuffing
• Small tapestry needle

NOTE: The finished project is very small and is not suitable for children ages three and under.

legs
With A, cast on 4 stitches onto one DPN.

RND 1 (WORK AS AN I-CORD): [Kfb] 4 times (8 sts).

Divide the stitches onto 2 DPNs to continue working in a round.

RNDS 2 AND 3: Knit.

Break the yarn and set the stitches aside on the needles.

Make another leg in the same way as the first, without breaking the yarn.

join legs
Place the stitches of the first leg that you knit onto the working needles, so that the first 4 stitches of each leg are on the DPN in front and the last 4 stitches of each leg are on the DPN in back, and the working yarn is attached to the rightmost stitch on the back needle.

To get ready to join the legs, place the first 4 stitches of each leg on the front DPN and the last 4 stitches of each leg on the back DPN, with the working yarn attached to the rightmost stitch on the back DPN.

RND 4: Knit one round, joining the legs together as you knit (16 sts).

body
Distribute the stitches onto 3 DPNs to continue working in a round.

RND 5: [Kfb, k1] 8 times (24 sts).

RNDS 6 AND 7: Knit.

Break A, and switch to B and C.

RNDS 8–12: [K1B, k1C] to end (5 rnds).

Break C.

RND 13: Knit with B.

Switch to A (and break B).

RND 14: [K2tog, k2] 6 times (18 sts).

RND 15: Knit.

RND 16: K4, yo, k8, k2tog, k4 (18 sts).

RNDS 17–20: Knit (4 rnds).

Stuff the piece.

RND 21: [K2tog, k1] 6 times (12 sts).

RND 22: [K2tog] 6 times (6 sts).

Break the yarn and draw it tightly through the stitches with a tapestry needle.

With black, embroider eyes with 2 small stitches for each one, placed 2 stitches up from the yarn-over hole and spaced 3 stitches apart (with the yarn-over hole centered below these 3 stitches).

trunk
With A, cast on 4 stitches onto one DPN.

Knit 8 rows as an I-cord.

Break the yarn and draw it tightly through the stitches with a tapestry needle.

With the tail still threaded on the tapestry needle, insert the tip of the I-cord into the yarn-over hole, and pull it partially inside. Secure the I-cord in place by making several loose stitches through the head.

ears (make 2)
Turn the body on its side, and pick up and knit 5 stitches along the side of the head, placing them so that the bottom stitch is just above the last color change on the body. You will work these stitches flat.

To begin making an ear, pick up 5 vertical stitches along one side of the head.

ROW 1: K1, kfb, k1, kfb, k1 (7 sts).

ROWS 2–4: Knit (3 rows).

ROW 5: K1, k2tog, k1, k2tog, k1 (5 sts).

ROW 6: K2tog, k1, k2tog (3 sts).

Bind off the stitches.

arms (make 2)

Turn the body upside down, and pick up and knit 2 stitches, placed 2 stitches under one ear. You will work these stitches as an I-cord.

To begin making an arm, pick up and knit 2 horizontal stitches below one ear.

RND 1: [Kfb] twice (4 sts).

RNDS 2–5: Knit 4 rows as an I-cord.

Break the yarn and draw it tightly through the stitches with a tapestry needle.

beanie

With D, cast on 16 stitches onto 3 DPNs and join to work in a round.

You will incorporate E beginning in the first round.

RNDS 1–3: [K2D, k2E] to end.

RND 4: [K2togD, k2togE] 4 times (8 sts).

Break the yarns and draw them both tightly through the stitches with a tapestry needle.

finishing

Weave in all the remaining loose ends, stitching up the gap between the legs as you do so.

Place the cast-on edge of the beanie on top of the head, and tack in place with a few small stitches. Cut 2 pieces of D and weave them through the top of the beanie. Trim the strands to about ¼" (6mm) long, and carefully tease them out to make a fluffy pompom.

finished size

- 4¾" (12cm) wide by 5¼" (13.5cm) long by 9" (23cm) tall (not including flag)

special techniques

- Back stitch
- Kitchener stitch
- Mattress stitch
- Stranded color knitting

yarn

- Worsted-weight yarn in 2 colors, plus small amount of a contrasting color **4**
- Sample knit with Cascade 220, 100% wool, 3½ oz (100g), 220 yds (200m) in 8505 White **(A)**, 7814 Chartreuse **(B)**, and 7802 Cerise

other supplies

- Set of 7" size 5 US (3.75mm) double-pointed needles
- Size 5 US (3.75mm) circular needle (any length)
- Empty cube-shaped tissue box measuring approximately 4¼" long x 4¼" wide x 5" tall (11cm x 11cm x 12.5cm) when turned on its side with the perforated opening oriented vertically and facing front
- Small tapestry needle
- Fabric glue
- Straight pins
- Stuffing
- Two size 12mm safety eyes

gauge

- 2" (5cm) = 11 stitches and 15½ rows in St st
- 2" (5cm) = 11 stitches and 22 rows in garter st

NOTES: The flag and safety eyes are very small and are not suitable for children ages three and under. • If you are starting with a new or partially used box of tissues, remove the tissues by opening the box on one of the glued sides, then taping the box back up once it's empty. • The Base and Sides pieces are designed so that you can easily add or subtract stitches to fit your box; size adjustments to the top must be made by changing needle size. • When the pattern instructs you to keep colors consistent, that means you should work every stitch in the same color as you worked it in the previous round.

preparation

Turn the box on its side, so that the opening is oriented vertically and faces front.

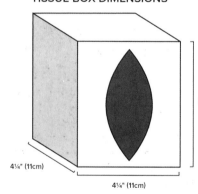

TISSUE BOX DIMENSIONS

4¼" (11cm)

4¼" (11cm)

5" (12.5cm)

base

With A, cast on 25 stitches onto one DPN to work flat. (This should fit the width of the box; adjust your stitch count if necessary.)

Knit 50 rows of garter stitch, or as many as needed to fit the length of the box (covering the base entirely).

NEXT ROW: Purl.

Knit 50 more rows.

Bind off all stitches.

sides

With A, cast on 24 stitches onto one DPN to work flat. (This should fit the height of the box; adjust your stitch count if necessary.)

Beginning with a purl row, work 9 rows of St st.

Switch to B (without breaking A), and work 4 rows of St st.

Switch to A (without breaking B), and work 4 rows of St st.

Repeat the above 8 rows 6 more times, so that you have 8 stripes of A and 7 stripes of B.

Switch to B (and break A), and purl one more row.

Break the yarn, leaving a tail of 24" (61cm), and set the stitches aside on the needle.

Make another piece in the same way as the first, without breaking the yarn.

When both pieces are complete, tack them together at one corner of the cast-on edges—this will be the top of the tent's opening. Wrap the pieces around your box to make sure you have the correct length. (It should fit snugly around the box, and pull just a bit at the tent's opening.) If you need to, add rows to the piece with the working yarn attached. (Don't worry about the width of the stripes, since they will be hidden at the back of the piece.)

After you have made the 2 side pieces, attach their cast-on edges at one corner, and check the fit around the box before seaming them together.

Once you are happy with the length, hold the DPNs together so that the purl sides of the pieces face each other, and seam with Kitchener stitch.

top

NOTE: The cast-on edge of this piece should be able to fit snugly around the top of the box. If you need to make adjustments, change your needle size as you would when checking gauge.

With B, cast on 88 stitches onto the circular needle. Join, being careful not to twist the stitches.

RNDS 1–4: Purl.

RND 5: [P2tog, p9] 8 times (80 sts).

RNDS 6–11: [K5B, k5A] to end (6 rnds).

RND 12: Keeping colors consistent, [k2, k2tog, k1] 16 times (64 sts).

RNDS 13–18: [K4B, k4A] to end (6 rnds).

RND 19: Keeping colors consistent, [k1, k2tog, k1] 16 times (48 sts).

Switch to DPNs now or whenever they are more comfortable.

RNDS 20–24: [K3B, k3A] to end (5 rnds).

RND 25: Keeping colors consistent, [k1, k2tog] 16 times (32 sts).

RNDS 26–29: [K2B, k2A] to end (4 rnds).

RND 30: Keeping colors consistent, [k2tog] 16 times (16 sts).

RNDS 31–34: [K1B, k1A] to end (4 rnds).

RND 35: With B only, [k2tog] 8 times (8 sts).

Break the yarns and draw them both tightly through the stitches with a tapestry needle.

flag

With a contrasting color, cast on 10 stitches onto one DPN to work flat.

ROWS 1–3: Knit.

ROW 4: K2tog, k6, k2tog (8 sts).

ROWS 5–7: Knit (3 rows).

ROW 8: K2tog, k4, k2tog (6 sts).

ROWS 9–11: Knit (3 rows).

ROW 12: K2tog, k2, k2tog (4 sts).

ROWS 13–15: Knit (3 rows).

ROW 16: [K2tog] twice (2 sts).

ROWS 17–19: Knit (3 rows).

Break the yarn and draw it tightly through the stitches with a tapestry needle.

pole

With A, cast on 2 stitches onto one DPN, leaving a tail for attaching.

Knit 12 rows of I-cord, then break the yarn and draw it tightly through the stitches with a tapestry needle.

Place the cast-on edge of the flag against the pole, and stitch it in place with mattress stitch.

finishing

Cut a slit at the bottom front of the box so that the base can fit inside and wrap it around the outside, with the knit stitches facing the box along the edge.

Use a small amount of fabric glue to secure the inside half of the base piece to the inside bottom of the box.

Place the side piece around the box, with the flaps centered at the front opening and flaring out at the bottom. You will seam the bottom edge of the side piece (except for the flaps) to the bottom half of the base piece using mattress stitch. Begin stitching about 1" (2.5cm) from the corner on the front of the box, then stitch around 3 sides, and finish by stitching along 1" (2.5cm) at the opposite corner of the front of the box.

If your stripes on the top piece look three-dimensional, grasp the piece on opposite sides and stretch it to even out the tension. Repeat this in several areas until the stripes lie flat.

Place the top piece over the top of the box. Pull its cast-on edge down at each of the four corners and pin it in place, overlapping 6 stitches on the side piece. Next, pull the middle of the front edge down onto the tent's opening, and pin in place. Reach under the top piece and insert stuffing—you want to fill out the piece while letting it retain a tentlike shape. When you are happy with the amount of stuffing, pull down the middle of the top on the remaining 3 sides and pin in place.

Next, attach the top piece to the sides, using back stitch. Remove the pins as you come to them. Follow the wavy contour that should have resulted from your pulling and pinning.

Use back stitch to secure the top over the side piece, following the wavy pinned-out shape.

Carefully cut away the areas on the box that are visible under the tent flaps, making sure to leave the rest of the cardboard intact.

Attach the flagpole to the top of the tent using mattress stitch—stitch all the way around the tiny pole to make it stand up.

Weave in the loose ends.

Hold the eyes up to either side of the flaps. Once you have decided on their placement (in the sample, 4 stitches down from the top piece and 6 stitches from the side piece's cast-on edge), carefully poke holes into the box for the eye shafts to go in. Place the eyes in the holes, then attach the back pieces on the inside of the box.

A-1 the Blimp

finished size
• 5½" (14cm) long

special techniques
• Kitchener stitch
• Mattress stitch
• Picking up stitches
• Stranded color knitting

yarn
• Worsted-weight yarn in 4 colors [4]
• Sample knit with Cascade 220, 100% wool, 3½ oz (100g), 220 yds (200m) in 8505 White **(A)**, 9469 Hot Pink **(B)**, 9542 Blaze **(C)**, and 9421 Blue Hawaii **(D)**

other supplies
• Set of size 5 US (3.75mm) double-pointed needles
• Small amount of stuffing
• Small tapestry needle
• Two size 9mm safety eyes

NOTES: If you're knitting for a child ages three or under, replace the safety eyes with embroidered eyes. • When the pattern instructs you to keep colors consistent, that means you should work every stitch in the same color as you worked it in the previous round.

body
With A, cast on 4 stitches onto one DPN.

RND 1 (WORK AS AN I-CORD): [Kfb] 4 times (8 sts).

Distribute the stitches onto 3 DPNs to continue working in a round.

RND 2: [K1A, k1B] to end.

RND 3: Keeping colors consistent, [Kfb] 8 times (16 sts).

RNDS 4–7: [K2A, k2B] to end (4 rnds).

RND 8: Keeping colors consistent, [k1, m1, k1] 8 times (24 sts).

RNDS 9–12: [K3A, k3B] to end (4 rnds).

RND 13: Keeping colors consistent, [k1, m1, k2] 8 times (32 sts).

RNDS 14 AND 15: [K4A, k4B] to end.

RND 16: Keeping colors consistent, [k2, m1, k2] 8 times (40 sts).

RNDS 17–26: [K5A, k5B] to end (10 rnds).

RND 27: Keeping colors consistent, [k2, k2tog, k1] 8 times (32 sts).

RND 28: [K4A, k4B] to end.

Switch to C.

RND 29: Knit.

RND 30: K1, [k2tog, k2] to last 3 sts, k2tog, k1 (24 sts).

RNDS 31 AND 32: Knit.

Stuff the piece. If your stripes look three-dimensional, grasp the piece on either side and stretch it to even out the tension. Repeat this

in several areas until the stripes lie flat.

Attach the eyes, placing them 3 stripes apart and 3 stitches back from the last color change.

RND 33: [K2tog, k1] 8 times (16 sts).

RND 34: Knit.

If necessary, add more stuffing to the top.

RND 35: [K2tog] 8 times (8 sts).

Break the yarn and draw it tightly through the stitches with a tapestry needle.

fins
Hold the body so that the skinny end is on the right, and with A, pick up and knit 8 stitches on the top stripe of A, starting at the tip of the tail. You will work these stitches flat.

To begin making a fin, pick up and knit 8 stitches, starting at the skinny tip of the body.

ROWS 1 AND 2: Knit.

ROW 3: K1, ssk, k5 (7 sts).

ROW 4: Knit.

ROW 5: K1, ssk, k4 (6 sts).

ROW 6: Knit.

ROW 7: K1, ssk, k3 (5 sts).

ROW 8: Knit.

ROW 9: K1, ssk, k2 (4 sts).

ROW 10: Knit.

ROW 11: [Ssk] twice, then pass the first stitch over the second to bind off.

Make 2 more fins in the same way, placing them on the lower edges of the two side stripes of A, so that they are evenly spaced.

gondola

With D, cast on 16 stitches onto 3 DPNs, leaving a tail for attaching, and join to work in a round.

RNDS 1–4: Knit.

RND 5: K2tog, k4, [k2tog] twice, k4, k2tog (12 sts).

RND 6: K2tog, k2, [k2tog] twice, k2, k2tog (8 sts).

Divide the stitches onto 2 DPNs and bind off using Kitchener stitch.

finishing

Stuff the gondola and attach its cast-on edge to the bottom of the blimp with mattress stitch.

With A, embroider windows onto the sides of the gondola with 2 small horizontal stitches for each.

Weave in the loose ends.

With D, embroider a name or number onto the side stripes of A.

Smallish Sun

finished size

- 3½" (9cm) in diameter

special technique

- Picking up stitches

yarn

- Worsted-weight yarn in 2 colors 4

- Sample knit with Cascade 220, 100% wool, 3½ oz (100g), 220 yds (200m) in 7828 Neon Yellow **(A)** and 9463B Gold **(B)**

other supplies

- Set of size 5 US (3.75mm) double-pointed needles

- Small amount of stuffing

- Small tapestry needle

- Two size 6mm safety eyes

NOTE: If you're knitting for a child ages three or under, replace the safety eyes with embroidered eyes.

body

With A, cast on 4 stitches onto one DPN.

RND 1 (WORK AS AN I-CORD): [Kfb] 4 times (8 sts).

Distribute the stitches onto 3 DPNs to continue working in a round.

RND 2: [Kfb] 8 times (16 sts).

RND 3: Knit.

RND 4: [Kfb, k1] 8 times (24 sts).

RND 5: Knit.

RND 6: [Kfb, k2] 8 times (32 sts).

RND 7: Knit.

RND 8: [Kfb, k3] 8 times (40 sts).

RND 9: Knit.

RND 10: Purl.

RNDS 11 AND 12: Knit.

RND 13: [K2tog, k3] 8 times (32 sts).

RND 14: Knit.

RND 15: [K2tog, k2] 8 times (24 sts).

RND 16: Knit.

RND 17: [K2tog, k1] 8 times (16 sts).

RND 18: Knit.

Stuff the piece.

RND 19: [K2tog] 8 times (8 sts).

Break the yarn and draw it loosely through the stitches with a tapestry needle. Reach inside to attach the eyes, placing them 2 stitches from the opening and spaced 4 stitches apart. Once you have attached the eyes, cinch the stitches closed.

Weave in the loose ends.

rays

Hold the body with the eyes facing you, and with B, pick up and knit 4 horizontal stitches along the purl round. (Pick up the row of bumps that is closer to you.) You will work these stitches flat.

To begin making a ray, pick up and knit 4 stitches along the outside edge of the piece.

ROWS 1–3: Knit.

ROW 4: [K2tog] twice (2 sts).

ROW 5: Knit.

Break the yarn and draw it tightly through the stitches with a tapestry needle.

Rotate the piece 180 degrees, and pick up and knit 4 stitches directly opposite the first ray.

Work the same as the first ray.

For the third ray, rotate the piece 90 degrees, and pick up and knit 4 stitches midway between the first two rays. The fourth ray should be placed opposite this one.

After making 4 rays, weave in all loose ends.

Pick up and knit the last 4 rays in the spaces between the existing rays.

finishing

Weave in the remaining loose ends.

Rainbowbird

finished size

• 3" (7.5cm) long (from beak to tail)

special techniques

• Picking up stitches
• Stranded color knitting

yarn

• Fingering-weight yarn in 7 rainbow colors, plus small amount of black **1**

• Samples knit with Knit Picks Palette, 100% wool, 1¾ oz (50g), 231 yds (211m) in Lady Slipper **(A)**, Majestic **(B)**, Cyan **(C)**, Peapod **(D)**, Canary **(E)**, Orange **(F)**, Serrano **(G)**, and Black **(H)**

other supplies

• Set of size 1 US (2.25mm) double-pointed needles

• Small amount of stuffing

• Small tapestry needle

NOTES: The finished project is very small and is not suitable for children ages three and under. • Leave the yarn tails resulting from color changes inside the piece as you go, pulling them tightly after knitting a few rounds in a new color.

body (worked back to front)

With A, cast on 3 stitches onto one DPN.

RND 1 (WORK AS AN I-CORD): Knit.

RND 2 (WORK AS AN I-CORD): [Kfb] 3 times (6 sts).

Divide the stitches onto 3 DPNs to continue working in a round.

RND 3: Knit.

RND 4: [Kfb, k1] 3 times (9 sts).

RND 5: [K1B, k2A] to end.

Switch to B only.

RND 6: [Kfb, k2] 3 times (12 sts).

RND 7: Knit.

RND 8: [Kfb, k1] 6 times (18 sts).

RND 9: Knit.

RND 10: [Kfb, k2] 6 times (24 sts).

RND 11: [K1C, k2B] to end.

Switch to C only.

RNDS 12–16: Knit (5 rnds).

RND 17: [K1D, k2C] to end.

Switch to D only.

RND 18: Knit.

RND 19: [K2tog, k2] 6 times (18 sts).

RND 20: Knit.

RND 21: [K2tog, k1] 6 times (12 sts).

Stuff the piece before continuing.

neck

Transfer the stitches onto 2 DPNs for this section. As you work the neck, stuff the tails of yarn inside the piece as you go to help fill out the piece.

RND 22: [K2tog] 6 times (6 sts).

RND 23: [K1E, k1D] to end.

Switch to E only.

RNDS 24–28: Knit (5 rnds).

RND 29: [K1F, k1E] to end.

Switch to F only.

RNDS 30–34: Knit (5 rnds).

RND 35: [K1G, k1F] to end.

Switch to G only.

RND 36: Knit.

head

RND 37: [Kfb] 6 times (12 sts).

Distribute the stitches back onto 3 DPNs to continue working in a round. If the neck seems understuffed with the yarn tails only, add a small amount of stuffing to it now.

RNDS 38–42: Knit (5 rnds).

Switch to E.

RND 43: [K2tog, k1] 4 times (8 sts).

RNDS 44 AND 45: Knit.

Insert a pinch of stuffing into the head section.

Switch to H. (You can leave the tails resulting from this color change on the outside of the piece to weave in later.)

RND 46: [K2tog] 4 times (4 sts).

Place the stitches onto one DPN to work as an I-cord.

RND 47: Knit.

RND 48: [K2tog] twice (2 sts).

Break the yarn and draw it tightly through the stitches with a tapestry needle.

With black, embroider the eyes with 2 small horizontal stitches for each on either side of the head, placed 3 stitches back from the G-to-E color change and spaced 4 stitches apart.

right wing

Turn the body upside down with the head pointing to the left. With C, pick up and knit 6 stitches on the C section at the side of the body, aligned with the eye. You will work these stitches flat.

ROW 1: Purl.

ROW 2: Knit.

ROW 3: Purl.

Switch to B.

ROW 4: Knit.

ROW 5: Purl.

ROW 6: K4, k2tog (5 sts).

ROW 7: Purl.

Switch to A.

ROW 8: K3, k2tog (4 sts).

ROW 9: Purl.

ROW 10: Knit.

ROW 11: [P2tog] twice (2 sts).

Break the yarn and draw it tightly through the stitches with a tapestry needle from right to left.

Pick up stitches for the right wings. Pick up stitches in the opposite direction for the left wing.

left wing

Turn the body upside down with the head pointing to the right. With A, pick up and knit 6 stitches directly opposite the right wing.

ROW 1: Purl.

ROW 2: Knit.

ROW 3: Purl.

Switch to B.

ROW 4: Knit.

ROW 5: Purl.

ROW 6: K2tog, k4 (5 sts).

ROW 7: Purl.

Switch to A.

ROW 8: K2tog, k3 (4 sts).

ROW 9: Purl.

ROW 10: Knit.

ROW 11: [P2tog] twice (2 sts).

Break the yarn and draw it tightly through the stitches with a tapestry needle from right to left.

legs (make 2)

Turn the body upside down with the head facing you. With C, pick up and knit 2 stitches, placed about 4 stitches to the inside of one of the wings. (When finished, the legs should be spaced about 3 stitches apart.)

ROWS 1–10: Knit as an I-cord.

Turn to work the piece flat.

ROW 11: [Kfb] twice (4 sts).

ROW 12: Knit.

ROW 13: Knit.

Bind off the stitches.

finishing

Weave in the remaining loose ends. If you would like your rainbowbird to hold a pose, pinch the body in place as you would like it, and use the loose ends to stitch it in place as you weave them in.

Tiny Kite

finished size
- 2½" (6.5cm) tall (not including tail or string)

special techniques
- Intarsia
- Mattress stitch

yarn
- Fingering-weight yarn in 2 colors, plus small amounts of white and black
- Sample knit with Cascade Heritage, 75% wool, 25% nylon, 3½ oz (100g), 437 yds (399.5m) in 5626 Turquoise **(A)**, 5641 Mango **(B)**, 5618 Snow, and 5672 Real Black

other supplies
- Pair of size 1 US (2.25mm) double-pointed needles
- Small tapestry needle
- Small amount of stuffing

NOTES: The finished project is very small and is not suitable for children ages three and under. • This project is worked flat on 2 needles. If you prefer, you can substitute 2 straight needles for the DPNs. • When the pattern instructs you to keep colors consistent, that means you should work every stitch in the same color as you worked it in the previous row.

sides (make 2)

With A, cast on 2 stitches. Then with B, cast on 2 more stitches adjacent to the first 2.

Each time you switch colors, work one stitch with the new color, then twist the working yarn of the old color once around the new color before working the second stitch in the new color.

ROW 1: P2B, p2A.

ROW 2: Keeping colors consistent, [k1, m1, k1] twice (6 sts).

ROW 3: P3B, p3A.

ROW 4: K3A, k3B.

ROW 5: P3B, p3A.

ROW 6: Keeping colors consistent, k1, m1, k2, k2, m1, k1 (8 sts).

ROW 7: P4B, p4A.

ROW 8: Keeping colors consistent, k1, m1, k3, k3, m1, k1 (10 sts).

ROW 9: P5B, p5A.

ROW 10: Keeping colors consistent, k1, m1, k4, k4, m1, k1 (12 sts).

ROW 11: P6B, p6A.

ROW 12: Keeping colors consistent, k1, m1, k5, k5, m1, k1 (14 sts).

ROW 13: P7B, p7A.

ROW 14: Keeping colors consistent, k1, m1, k6, k6, m1, k1 (16 sts).

ROW 15: P8B, p8A.

ROW 16: Keeping colors consistent, k1, m1, k7, k7, m1, k1 (18 sts).

ROW 17: P9B, p9A.

ROW 18: Keeping colors consistent, k1, m1, k8, k8, m1, k1 (20 sts).

Break the yarns. You will swap the colors beginning in the next row.

ROW 19: P10A, p10B.

ROW 20: Keeping colors consistent, k1, [k2tog] twice, k5, k5, [ssk] twice, k1 (16 sts).

ROW 21: P8A, p8B.

ROW 22: Keeping colors consistent, k1, k2tog, k5, k5, ssk, k1 (14 sts).

ROW 23: P7A, p7B.

ROW 24: Keeping colors consistent, k1, k2tog, k4, k4, ssk, k1 (12 sts).

ROW 25: P6A, p6B.

ROW 26: Keeping colors consistent, k1, k2tog, k3, k3, ssk, k1 (10 sts).

ROW 27: P5A, p5B.

ROW 28: Keeping colors consistent, k1, k2tog, k2, k2, ssk, k1 (8 sts).

ROW 29: P4A, p4B.

ROW 30: Keeping colors consistent, k1, k2tog, k1, k1, ssk, k1 (6 sts).

ROW 31: P3A, p3B.

ROW 32: Keeping colors consistent, k1, k2tog, ssk, k1 (4 sts).

ROW 33: P2A, p2B.

ROW 34: K2togA, sskB.

Break the yarns and set the stitches aside on a spare needle.

finishing

Place the stitches of both pieces adjacent to each other on one needle, with the knit stitches facing forward.

Thread the tail attached to the leftmost stitch on a tapestry needle, then draw the yarn tightly through the stitches from left to right. You can weave in the rest of the tails after seaming together the edges.

Place the purl sides of the 2 pieces

against each other, and seam the side edges together, using mattress stitch. Leave the piece unstuffed.

Weave in the remaining loose ends.

With black, embroider eyes with 2 small horizontal stitches for each, placed just below the color change and spaced 4 stitches apart.

For the tail, cut a 4" (10cm) piece of white yarn and six 4" (10cm) pieces of B. Attach the white yarn to the bottom tip of the kite, and tie the pieces of B tightly around it, using double knots. Space them out evenly. Trim the pieces of B to ¼" (6mm).

For the string, cut a 12" (30.5cm) piece of white yarn and attach it to the middle back of the piece.

finished size

• 3" (7.5cm) long

yarn

• Fingering-weight yarn in one color, plus small amount of black [1]

• Sample knit with Knit Picks Palette, 100% wool, 1¾ oz (50g), 231 yds (211m) in White and Black

other supplies

• Set of size 1 US (2.25mm) double-pointed needles

• Small amount of stuffing

• Small tapestry needle

NOTE: The finished project is very small and is not suitable for children ages three and under.

cloud

Cast on 6 sts onto 2 DPNs and join to work in a round.

RND 1: [Kfb] 6 times (12 sts).

RND 2: [Kfb, k1] 6 times (18 sts).

Distribute the stitches onto 3 DPNs to continue working in a round.

RND 3: Knit.

RND 4: [Kfb] twice, k to last 2 sts, [kfb] twice (22 sts).

RND 5: Knit.

RND 6: [Kfb] twice, k to last 2 sts, [kfb] twice (26 sts).

RND 7: Knit.

RND 8: Kfb, k to last st, kfb (28 sts).

RND 9: Knit.

RND 10: Kfb, k to last st, kfb (30 sts).

RNDS 11–16: Knit (6 rnds).

RND 17: K2tog, k to last 2 sts, k2tog (28 sts).

RND 18: Knit.

RND 19: [K2tog] twice, k to last 4 sts, [k2tog] twice (24 sts).

RND 20: Knit.

RND 21: [K2tog] twice, k to last 4 sts, [k2tog] twice (20 sts).

RND 22: [Kfb] twice, k to last 2 sts, [kfb] twice (24 sts).

RND 23: Knit.

RND 24: Kfb, k to last st, kfb (26 sts).

RNDS 25–28: Knit (4 rnds).

RND 29: K2tog, k to last 2 sts, k2tog (24 sts).

RND 30: Knit.

RND 31: [K2tog] twice, k to last 4 sts, [k2tog] twice (20 sts).

RND 32: Knit.

RND 33: [K2tog] twice, k to last 4 sts, [k2tog] twice (16 sts).

RND 34: [Kfb] twice, k to last 2 sts, [kfb] twice (20 sts).

RNDS 35–38: Knit (4 rnds).

RND 39: K2tog, k to last 2 sts, k2tog (18 sts).

RND 40: Knit.

Stuff the piece.

RND 41: [K2tog, k1] 6 times (12 sts).

RND 42: [K2tog] 6 times (6 sts).

Break the yarn and draw it tightly through the stitches with a tapestry needle.

finishing

Hold the cloud so that the bumps are at the top and, with black, embroider the eyes with 2 small vertical stitches for each, placed midway up one side and spaced 7 stitches apart.

Weave in the loose ends.

New to Knitting?

Never tried knitting before? Welcome to a world of crafty fun! The patterns contained in this book are ideal for knitters with some experience, but newbies who are up for a challenge can certainly tackle them, too. I recommend that new knitters use thicker yarn and bigger needles for the tinier projects in this book. They'll turn out the same, only a bit bigger!

MATERIALS

These are the basic materials and tools that you'll need to make the projects in this book.

yarn

Any yarn will do! That's especially true for toys. Use the yarn recommended in the patterns, use scrap yarn that you have in your stash, or even unravel an ugly sweater and repurpose its yarn.

needles

I recommend a set of four or five double-pointed needles (DPNs) for all the projects in this book, but a circular needle and the magic loop technique *(see Using a Circular Needle and the Magic Loop Technique, page 134)* will also work in most cases. Both DPNs and circular needles can take the place of straight needles when you're working a flat piece. Choose a needle size that will give you a relatively tight gauge, so

that the stuffing doesn't show between the stitches of the finished toy. This usually means choosing a needle two to three sizes smaller than the needle size recommended on the yarn label.

stuffing

I prefer polyester stuffing (aka polyfill) for easy use and care. It's also best for projects that require pulling knit pieces through the stuffing for arms and other appendages.

eyes

The easiest way to make eyes is to embroider them with a contrasting-color yarn. But you can also use buttons, beads, pieces of felt, or safety eyes with backs that snap in place.

TOOLS

A **tapestry needle** is like a large sewing needle for use with yarn. Use it to weave in the loose ends on your projects.

Scissors are handy for cutting and also (with the blades closed) getting stuffing into tight spaces. Choose a small pair with pointed tips for the most control.

A **crochet hook** can be useful for attaching hair to a toy or to pick up stitches that you accidentally dropped. Use one that's the same size as your knitting needles.

Straight pins are helpful when you need to attach larger pieces to each other; they can act as a stitching guide.

Stitch markers are little rings that help keep track of where a new round begins and ends. Slip one onto your needles between two stitches.

A **stitch counter** can help you remember how many rows or rounds you have worked.

skip the gauge check

I don't recommend checking gauge before beginning most toy projects: it's more fun to just get started! For larger projects that incorporate fixed sizes (like the Carnival Tent), checking gauge is a good idea, however. Find out how at **www.mochimochiland.com/how-to.**

TOY KNITTING BASICS

If you are a beginning knitter, you can refer to the Knitting Essentials on pages 138–142.

knitting with four DPNs

Double-pointed needles (DPNs) allow you to knit three-dimensional pieces in various shapes and sizes. The standard way to use them is to place your stitches onto three DPNs and knit with a fourth DPN.

1. Cast all the stitches onto one DPN, then distribute the stitches onto 3 DPNs by slipping them purlwise (right to left in the front loop) onto the other needles. Hold the DPNs so that the working yarn is attached to the top stitch on the right needle. To make sure you aren't twisting the stitches, align the bumpy cast-on edge to the insides of the needles.

2. Use a fourth needle to knit the stitches on the DPN in your left hand. Pull the yarn tightly between the needles to keep the first stitch from becoming too loose. When you finish knitting from the needle in your left hand, rotate the needles slightly in a clockwise direction, and continue knitting the stitches from the next needle onto your newly empty needle. When you reach the tail of the yarn (left from casting on), you have completed one round of knitting. Continue to the following needle to begin the next round.

3. Keep knitting from the needle in your left hand to the needle in your right, around and around. After knitting a few rounds, you will see a tube of knitting take shape.

knitting with two DPNs (as an I-cord)

Use this option when beginning the closed end of a piece or when working with four or fewer stitches.

After casting on, leave your stitches on just one DPN, and slide them to the right end of the needle (with the working yarn attached to the leftmost stitch). Pull the attached yarn behind the needle, and, pulling tightly, knit the first stitch onto a second needle. (In most patterns, you will work a kfb increase with this stitch.) Continue to work the rest of the stitches from the left needle onto the right.

Repeat this step, sliding the stitches to the right end of the needle again for each row/round. When you have increased the total number of stitches, you can distribute them onto two or three DPNs to continue working in a round.

knitting with three DPNs

This is an in-between technique for working with a number of stitches that is too large for two needles and too small for three.

1. Cast on the stitches and divide them onto two needles. Hold the needles parallel to each other, with the purl stitches facing each other and the working yarn attached to the rightmost stitch on the back needle.

2. With a third needle, knit into the first stitch on the front needle, then continue to knit the rest of the stitches on this needle.

When you have finished knitting these stitches, turn both needles around so that the cast-on tail is now attached to the leftmost stitch on the front needle. Continue in this way by turning the needles around each time you finish a needle.

using a circular needle and the magic loop technique

You can also work the patterns in this book using a circular needle and the magic loop technique, which allows you to work a variety of circumferences on one circular needle. This technique is ideal when knitting larger projects, like the Muffin Mountains and the Carnival Tent.

1. Cast on the specified number of stitches onto the needle, and slide them onto the flexible cable. Divide the stitches into two groups, and fold the cable in half between them, with the working yarn attached to the group on the bottom. Grasp the small section of the cable that lies between the two groups of stitches, and pull it out between the stitches until you have pulled out a big loop.

2. Slide the top group of stitches down to one end of the needle. Leave the bottom group of stitches on the cable, while keeping the loop pulled out between the two groups. Make sure that the bumpy cast-on edge is aligned to the inside. Pick up the empty end of the needle with your right hand, then knit the stitches from the left end of the needle onto the empty right end, pulling the yarn tightly to join the stitches into a round.

3. When you finish knitting the first group of stitches, slide the second group of stitches to the opposite end of the needle and slide the first group (which you just finished knitting) down onto the cable. Reverse their positions, and knit the second group of stitches to complete one round of knitting. Continue to repeat these steps to work multiple rounds.

stuffing and closing pieces

Most of the time, you will finish a piece by stuffing it and cinching the live stitches tightly together.

1. While the stitches are still on the needle, use your finger, the tip of a closed pair of scissors, or another small tool to insert enough stuffing into the piece. Use enough stuffing so that the piece's shape has definition, but not so much that the stuffing shows through between the stitches.

2. When you are finished knitting and ready to close the piece, cut the yarn, leaving a tail of a few inches or centimeters. Thread the tail onto a tapestry needle. Then, beginning with the first stitch in the round, insert the tapestry needle purlwise through each stitch, slipping the stitches off the needles as you go.

3. When you have slipped all the stitches off the needles, pull the tail tightly to draw the stitches closed.

weaving in loose ends

When you finish any of the projects in this book, you will be left with several loose ends of yarn sticking out everywhere. You can either weave these in as you go, or deal with them all at once as a last step when finishing your toy.

1. Thread the loose end onto a tapestry needle, and insert the needle back into the toy in the same place from which the tail emerges. (Not making a stitch in the knit fabric prevents the tail from pulling on the toy's surface and making it puckered.)

2. Bring the needle all the way out the other side of the toy. Repeat Steps 1 and 2 several more times to ensure that the tail is sufficiently caught in the stuffing on the inside of the piece and won't come loose.

3. When the end is sufficiently woven in, cut the yarn short, gently pressing on the toy so that the end will pop back and be hidden inside.

ADDING EYES

There are two types of eyes that I use for the projects in this book: embroidered eyes and safety eyes. Embroidered eyes are safe for small children as long as the piece that you're embroidering isn't itself a choking hazard. Safety eyes, despite their name, can pop out, so they should not be used on a toy for a small child.

embroidered eyes

Embroidering eyes on a toy gives you the most control over exactly what the eye will look like; you can make any shape, size, and color combination with embroidery. For the tiny projects in this book, I use just two small stitches of embroidery to make each eye.

1. Cut a piece of black yarn (or other contrasting-color yarn) of a few inches or centimeters. Thread the piece onto a tapestry needle, then stick the needle in one side of the toy and out the other side, just to the left of where you would like the eye to go. Make the first stitch of the eye, spanning half a knit stitch, and bring the needle out in the same place that you began the stitch. (To help make the eye rounder, split the black yarn when you bring the needle out for this stitch.)

2. Make another stitch in the same place as the first, to give the eye more volume and definition. This time, bring the needle out a few stitches away, to the left of where you would like the second eye to go. When you finish the second eye, bring the needle back out through the other side of the body.

safety eyes

For several of the larger projects in this book, I recommend using safety eyes. The trick is that the eyes come with backs that must be attached, so they need to be inserted before the piece is finished and closed up.

After you've stuffed the body, insert the front halves of the eyes where you would like them. Then reach inside the toy to snap the backs in place, with the flatter side of the backs facing the eye shaft.

I-CORD APPENDAGES

I-cords are thin tubes of circular knitting made using two double-pointed needles.

Because they are so skinny and flexible, they are versatile and can be used in different ways with tiny projects.

i-cord arms

One I-cord can become two arms when you insert it through the sides of a body and pull until an equal length sticks out from each side. Finish off the resulting loose ends by weaving them back through the arms and the body.

joining i-cord legs

Two I-cords can be joined together to make two parallel legs. After knitting the first I-cord, break the yarn and set

it aside. Make another I-cord without breaking the yarn. Get ready to join the I-cords into one round by placing the two needles parallel to each other, or by distributing the stitches differently onto the needles and holding them parallel as indicated in the pattern. You will use a third needle to work the following round. *(See Knitting with Three DPNs, page 133.)*

A similar technique can be used with a larger number of stitches, when the two I-cords are replaced by two tubes of circular knitting.

dividing a piece into i-cords

Conversely, a larger piece of knitting can be separated into two smaller I-cords for ears or other appendages. Work the first half of the stitches separately, leaving the other stitches on the needle to work later. After finishing off the first I-cord, break the yarn, leaving a long tail. (It should be long enough to complete a second I-cord.) Insert the

tail down through the I-cord and reattach it to the last live stitch to begin the second I-cord.

picking up stitches on a three-dimensional piece

Another way to add appendages without stitching them is to pick up stitches on the body, then work the stitches flat or in the round, depending on the shape of the appendage.

1. Decide where on the piece you want to pick up stitches. Depending on the orientation of the appendage, you may need to turn the piece sideways or upside down. Beginning with the rightmost stitch, slip the tip of a double-pointed needle under the bar between knit stitches, and place the yarn between the tip of the needle and the piece, with the loose end on the right.

2. Use the needle to pull a loop of yarn out from under the bar, creating a loop, as you would for a regular knit stitch.

3. For subsequent stitches, repeat Steps 1 and 2 with the bar immediately to the left on the body. If you are picking up stitches for a flat piece, pick up one stitch for every knit stitch. If you are picking up stitches for an I-cord, pick up the bars between each half of a stitch.

4. If the pattern calls for a vertical column of stitches to be picked up, use the same technique, except insert the needle through each knit stitch from the side.

picking up stitches around the perimeter of a piece

A seamless way to begin a box shape is to knit a flat piece, then pick up the stitches on the three remaining sides of the piece. This will prepare you to work the stitches in the round and build up the sides of the piece.

When you have finished the initial flat piece and are ready to pick up stitches, rotate the piece 90 degrees clockwise, so that the adjacent side faces up, then use a new double-pointed needle to pick up and knit the

stitches on this side, starting at the top right corner. Repeat this for each of the two remaining sides. When all sides have been picked up, you are ready to begin knitting in the round using a fifth double-pointed needle. Note that you will likely need to adjust for the difference between the number of side stitches and the number of stitches to be picked up by skipping every fourth or fifth stitch.

mattress stitch

One of the biggest challenges knitters have with toys is seaming pieces together. Mattress stitch is your friend—it's essentially a simple technique in which you stitch on the outside of the piece, and pull tightly to hide the seam. (For clarity, the photos shown here use a contrasting-color yarn for the stitching, and the stitches are very loose.)

The way you stitch two pieces together depends on the orientation of the stitches on the pieces.

If the vertical stitches run parallel to each other, slip the tapestry needle under two horizontal bars on one piece, then under the two corresponding bars on the other piece. Make your stitches back and forth in this way, and pull tightly to hide the seam.

If there are two horizontal rows of stitches to seam together (as in cast-on or bound-off edges), slip the tapestry needle under the V of each stitch, back and forth, and pull tightly to hide the seam.

When you encounter different combinations of these stitch orientations, just use the two stitch placements shown above, and adjust the

spacing of your stitches so that you have an even seam.

Although shown in two dimensions here, you can use mattress stitch in the same way with three-dimensional pieces.

back stitch

Back stitch is another seaming technique best used for joining two flat pieces together or attaching a flat piece to a three-dimensional piece. It can also be used on its own in a contrasting color for an embroidered line.

Overlap the two pieces. Insert the tapestry needle straight down through both pieces, and bring it back up some distance away. Insert the needle back down into the same place where you inserted it to begin with, so that the second stitch abuts the first. Continue to make stitches in this way, making your visible stitches a consistent length.

Knitting Essentials

If you're new to knitting or need a refresher course, you're in the right place.

cast on (CO)
Begin by estimating how long of a tail you need. The length will depend on the weight of the yarn and the size of the needles, but for most of the projects in this book, you can estimate ½" (13mm) per stitch, plus a few inches or centimeters for extra tail.

1. Make a slipknot with the yarn, slide the needle through the knot, and tighten. This will be the first stitch in the cast-on. Next, holding the needle in your right hand, grasp both ends of the yarn in the palm of your left hand. Wrap the yarn attached to the ball around the outside of your thumb, and the tail around the outside of your forefinger.

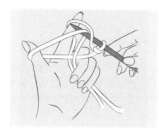

2. Insert the tip of the needle under the outer side of the yarn on your thumb from left to right.

3. With the yarn from your thumb still looped over the needle, bring the tip of the needle over the inner side of the yarn on your finger, and dip it around and under from right to left.

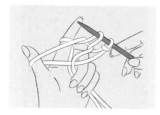

4. As you pull the needle under the yarn on your finger, bring the tip through the loop on your thumb. Let the yarn slip off your thumb, then insert your thumb back through the end of the yarn that's attached to the ball. As you do so, tighten the new stitch that's now on the needle.

Repeat Steps 2–4 until you have the required number of stitches on your needle.

knit (K)
1. Hold the needle with the stitches in your left hand, and the yarn attached to the rightmost stitch. Hold the empty needle in your right hand. (For subsequent stitches, the attached yarn will be on the right needle.) Insert the tip of the right needle under the front of the first stitch from left to right, and wrap the yarn around the tip of the right needle from left to right.

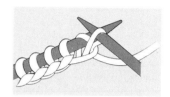

2. Pull the tip of the right needle down through the stitch on the left needle, pulling the wrapped yarn out with it.

3. Slip the stitch off the left needle. You now have a new stitch on the right needle.

purl (P)
The purl stitch is the reverse of the knit stitch; it happens automatically on the reverse side of knit stitches. When knitting a flat piece, you will usually turn the piece at the end of the row and work purl stitches on the reverse side.

1. Insert the tip of the right needle under the front of the first stitch on the left needle, from right to left. Wrap the working yarn from right to left around the tip of the right needle.

2. Pull the tip of the right needle down through the stitch on the left needle, pulling the wrapped yarn out with it before slipping the stitch off the left needle.

bind off (BO)

Use this technique to finish flat pieces. *(For finishing circular pieces, see Stuffing and Closing Pieces, page 134.)*

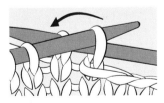

Knit the first two stitches normally. Slip the tip of the left needle into the first of those stitches from left to right, then slip the stitch over the second stitch and off the needle. Knit the next stitch on the left needle, and again slip the right stitch over the left. Repeat this until you are left with one stitch.

To finish off, break the yarn, slip the last stitch off the needle, and slip the loose end of the yarn through the stitch. Pull tightly to secure.

If a pattern calls for binding off the stitches on the purl side of a piece, bind them off in the same way, but purl all the stitches instead of knitting them.

knit through front and back of stitch (KFB)

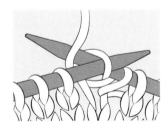

Knit a stitch normally, but without pulling the stitch off the left needle. Then knit into the same stitch again, this time inserting the tip of the right needle through the back half of the stitch. Once you pull the right needle and yarn through, slip the stitch off the left needle. This will increase the total number of stitches by one.

make 1 (M1)

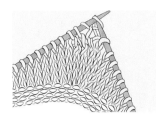

With the right needle, pick up the top bar that appears between the needles, and place it on the left needle. Knit this new stitch through the back loop, and slip it off the left needle.

knit 2 together (K2TOG)

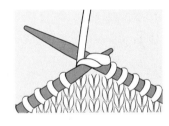

Insert the right needle under the first two stitches on the left needle. Wrap the yarn as you would normally do for a knit stitch, and slip both stitches off the left needle. This will decrease the total number of stitches by one.

purl 2 together (P2TOG)

Insert the tip of the right needle purlwise through the front of the first two stitches on the left needle. Wrap the yarn as you normally would for a purl stitch, pull it through, and slip both stitches off the left needle. This will decrease the total number of stitches by one.

slip, slip, knit together (SSK)

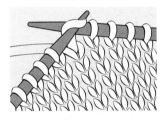

1. Insert the tip of the right needle through the front of a stitch as if to knit, and slip the stitch off the left needle without knitting. Repeat for the next stitch on the left needle. You now have two twisted stitches on the right needle.

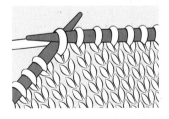

2. Slip both stitches back onto the left needle so that they remain twisted.

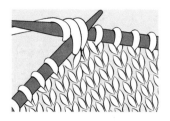

3. Insert the right needle through the backs of the two stitches on the left needle, and knit them together.

yarn over (YO)

Yarn over is an increase stitch that makes a small hole in your knitting.

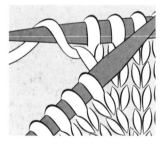

1. Bring the yarn around in front of the needle in your right hand, and wrap it on the needle from front to back.

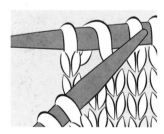

2. Knit the next stitch as you normally would, while keeping the extra loop on the right needle. You'll see a small gap where you added the loop.

joining new yarn

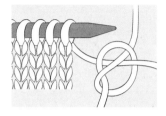

To join a new ball of yarn or a new color of yarn, tie the tail of the working yarn and the beginning of the new yarn together in a loose knot. Knit one stitch with the new yarn, then gently pull the knot tight and closer to the back or the wrong side of the piece.

Use this technique when a pattern calls for you to switch to a new yarn color and you won't be be using the first color again (or at least not again for a number of rows).

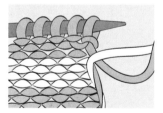

If you will use the first color again soon, as in a striped pattern of alternating colors, do not cut the first color; instead, wrap the yarns together when you start a new color, and carry the first color loosely up the side (in flat knitting) or inside (in circular knitting) of the piece until you will use it again.

intarsia color change

Intarsia is a technique used in flat knitting to create a color design other than a stripe, for which you need to switch colors mid-row.

1. After establishing the new color in a previous row (see Joining New Yarn, above), the yarn for the new color will already be attached when you come to it. Before knitting the first stitch in the new color, twist the two yarns together once on the back of the piece. This will prevent a gap from forming between the two colors.

2. When purling back across the same row, again wrap the yarns together before purling the first stitch in the other color.

stranded color knitting

Stranded color knitting (also known as Fair Isle) is a method of carrying multiple strands of different colors of yarn along the back of a piece as you knit in the round, incorporating the different colors in your stitches as you need them. Often there will be a chart to refer to for the color pattern.

It's important to keep a consistent, relatively loose tension when you're doing stranded color knitting, without pulling any stitches too tightly, so that the finished piece doesn't pucker.

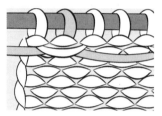

As you knit, you can either hold the two strands of yarn in different hands, or you can simply drop the color that you're not working with at the moment. If there are six or more consecutive stitches in one color, twist the other color once around the working yarn every few stitches to help maintain an even tension.

After knitting a round with multiple colors, you should see the yarns carried evenly across the backside of the piece.

wrap & turn (W+T)

The technique of wrap and turn lets you turn multiple times within a single row or round, thereby lengthening one area of a piece of knitting. This results in a bend in the knitting that's perfect for making a leg that bends into a foot.

The following illustrations show a wrap and turn on the knit side; a wrap and turn on the purl side is worked the same way.

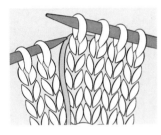

1. When you come to the stitch to be wrapped, slip it purlwise from the left needle onto the right, then bring the yarn forward to the front of the piece.

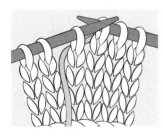

2. Slip the stitch back onto the left needle. You will next turn the knitting so that the purl side faces you, and the working yarn is connected to the last stitch on the right needle. Proceed to purl the stitches from the left needle onto the right.

kitchener stitch

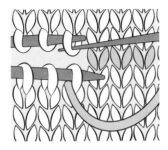

setup

Divide the stitches equally onto two needles. Hold the needles parallel to each other with the working yarn attached to the rightmost stitch of the back needle.

Cut the working yarn, leaving a long tail, and thread the tail onto a tapestry needle. Insert the tapestry needle purlwise through the first stitch on the front needle, without slipping the stitch off the needle. Pull the tail through.

Next, insert the tapestry needle knitwise through the first stitch on the back needle and pull the tail through, again without slipping the stitch off the needle.

seaming

1. Insert the tapestry needle knitwise through the first stitch on the front needle, and slip the stitch off the needle.

2. Insert the tapestry needle purlwise through the following stitch on the front needle, without slipping the stitch off the needle.

3. Insert the tapestry needle purlwise through the first stitch on the back needle, and slip the stitch off the needle.

4. Insert the tapestry needle knitwise through the following stitch on the back needle, without slipping the stitch off the needle.

Repeat steps 1-4, until only one stitch remains on each needle.

Insert the tapestry needle knitwise through the stitch on the front needle and slip it off, then insert the tapestry needle purlwise through the back needle and slip it off. Weave in the tail.

three-needle bind-off

Divide the stitches equally onto two needles. Hold the needles parallel to each other with the working yarn attached to the rightmost stitch of the back needle.

Using a third needle, knit the first stitch on the front needle and the first stitch on the back needle together. Knit together with the following stitches on each needle in the same way.

Next, slip the first (rightmost) stitch on the right needle over the second stitch, binding off the first stitch.

Continue this pattern until only one stitch remains on the right needle. To finish off, break the yarn, slip the stitch off the needle, and slip the loose end through the stitch. Pull tightly to secure.

crochet chain

Make a slipknot with the yarn, slide the hook through, and tighten. Next, wrap the end of the yarn attached to the ball around the shaft of the hook, from back to front. Use the hook to pull this yarn through the slipknot, slipping the knot off the hook as you do so.

Repeat this step, pulling the yarn through the existing loop on the hook and slipping the old loop off, until you have a chain that's as long as you want it. To finish, cut the yarn and pull it through the last loop.

KNITTING ABBREVIATIONS

[ ] Repeat actions within brackets as many times as specified in the number after the brackets

BO Bind off

CO Cast on

DPNS Double-pointed needles

K Knit

K2TOG Knit 2 stitches together

KFB Knit through the front and the back of one stitch

M1 Pick up the bar between two stitches and knit through its back loop

P Purl

P2TOG Purl 2 stitches together

RND(S) Round(s)

SSK Slip 2 stitches knitwise onto the right needle, then knit them together

ST(S) Stitch(es)

ST ST Stockinette stitch (knit on the right side, purl on the wrong side)

W+T Wrap and turn

YO yarn over

RESOURCES

yarn

CASCADE YARNS
www.cascadeyarns.com

KNIT PICKS
www.knitpicks.com

MADELINETOSH
www.madelinetosh.com

BERROCO
www.berroco.com

LION BRAND
www.lionbrand.com

stuffing
Stuffing can be found in larger craft stores and online.

JO-ANN FABRIC AND CRAFT STORES
www.joann.com

MICHAELS
www.michaels.com

eyes
Plastic safety eyes are available from a variety of online retailers.

HARVEY'S HOBBY HUT
www.harveyshobbyhut.com

YEAHSHOP
www.etsy.com/shop/yeahshop

6060
www.etsy.com/shop/6060

Turn the page for a backdrop you can use to photograph your own mochis.

Then share your snapshot with the world!

more adventures
Find more patterns, tips, and behind-the-scenes extras for this book at **www.mochimochiland.com/adventuresinmochimochiland**

Author's Note

Mochimochi Land is more than a setting for the stories in this book—it's the alternative reality that has taken over my work (and much of my life) since 2007. After writing four books of patterns for creatures who emerged from this realm, it is my great pleasure to write a book that shows for the first time in print what Mochimochi Land really looks like, at least in my own imagination. I hope that all ages of readers get a kick out of the stories; I hope that some of you will be inspired to take up the craft of knitting; and I hope that those of you who are already avid knitters will take the landscapes in these pages as inspiration for creating your own worlds.

Acknowledgments

More work than anyone could know went into the making of this book, and my gratitude runs deep for everyone who gave their time and talent to *Adventures in Mochimochi Land*.

As my photographer, Brandi went far beyond what was required to make magic out of my heaps of wool. As my friend, she helped me through some difficult moments. Her family members—Mike, Sonnie, and Sarah—all deserve medals for their patience and accommodation. I am certain that the spirit of Sonny Simons can be sensed within these pages.

Jessica Chace inspired the Joyful Oyster design in this book, and my thanks go to her for sharing her creativity.

I am grateful for my pattern testers, especially Rikke, Joan, Linda, Amanda, and Yvonne, for happily taking on extra projects with short notice and providing that last bit of steam needed to finish up the manuscript. Many thanks to Brent Perrotti and Joan Foster for their nimble fingers, which spent hours upon hours making samples big and small.

The instructions in this book are clear and user-friendly thanks to my tech editor, Marilyn Passmore, who knows my patterns better than I do and who continues to make me a better technical writer.

Big thanks go to the wonderful people at Cascade Yarns, Knit Picks, and Lion Brand for providing the essential stuff of which Mochimochi Land is made.

As always, my husband, John, saw me through each of the challenges that came with this project, without once batting an eye. My thanks and love go to him and to my parents, Gretchen and Mark, for their emotional and practical support.

I am indebted to my editor, Caitlin Harpin, for being open to new ideas, for believing in the concept of this book, and for putting in the hard work to make it happen. My thanks to Stephanie Huntwork and Ashley Tucker for their efforts to understand my vision and find just the right ways to express it.

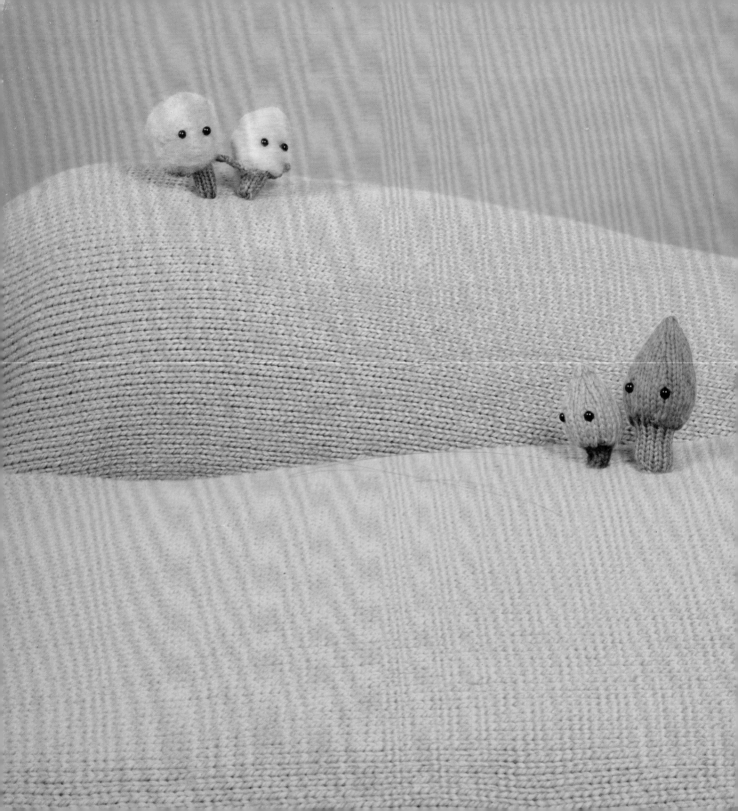